# GUIDES TO EDUCATIONAL MEDIA

4 TH EDITION

*Films*

*Filmstrips*

*Multimedia Kits*

*Programmed Instruction Materials*

*Recordings on Discs and Tapes*

*Slides*

*Transparencies*

*Videotapes*

MARGARET I. RUFSVOLD

*American Library Association*

*Chicago 1977*

Library of Congress Cataloging in Publication Data

Rufsvold, Margaret Irene, 1907-
　　Guides to educational media.

　　First-2d ed. published under title: Guides to
newer educational media.
　　Bibliography: p.
　　Includes index.
　　1. Audio-visual education—Bibliography.
2. Audio-visual materials—Catalogs. I. Title.
Z5814.V8R8 1977 [LB1043] 016.37133 77-5058
ISBN 0-8389-0232-4

Printed in the United States of America

# Contents

# Preface

The purpose of this fourth edition of Guides to Educational Media, like that of its predecessors, written in conjunction with Carolyn Guss and published in 1961, 1967, and 1971, is to identify and describe catalogs, indexes, lists, and reviewing services which systematically provide information about educational media. While the title, the purpose, and the criteria used in the compilation of the previous editions are retained in this edition, the work has been greatly enlarged, entirely rewritten, and slightly altered in scope for reasons which will be explained later.

This edition identifies and describes 245 educational media catalogs, indexes, and reviewing services; in addition, 35 related publications are mentioned in the annotations. The Guide is comprehensive within its scope rather than selective and provides information for all grade levels and audiences from preschool through university and adult levels including preservice and inservice professional groups. Several criteria were used, however, to establish scope parameters. These criteria were that the catalogs and lists should be: (1) published between January 1, 1972, and November 1, 1976; (2) separate publications with a considerable portion devoted to providing information about nonprint educational media; (3) available on a national basis to anyone interested in obtaining them; (4) published in the United States; and (5) designed to inform potential users concerning the availability and educational utility of one or more types of media.

Certain types of catalogs and lists have been excluded. These are: (1) the trade catalogs and promotional publications of producers/distributors which include only the materials produced and/or distributed by them; (2) catalogs of collections of audiovisual materials in universities, colleges, public libraries, and school systems; (3) catalogs of collections distributed by special interest groups such as denominational organizations; (4) catalogs from other countries and from international organizations not published in the United States; and (5) catalogs in preparation.

The term *educational media* as used in the earlier editions designated instructional materials which require special equipment and physical facilities. These types of media have continued to be the basic concern in this edition, namely 16mm and 8mm (regular and super) films and filmloops, 35mm filmstrips, 2" x 2" and 3¼" x 4" slides, audiotapes, videotapes, recordings, programmed and computer-assisted instructional materials, and transparencies. However, there are increasing numbers of multimedia indexes which include not only the types of media mentioned above and which require equipment but also a variety of other types of educational resources both printed and nonprinted: books, periodicals, maps, charts, globes, opaque pictures, dioramas, exhibits, realia, games, field trips, simulated activities, equipment, and special facilities or installations. These comprehensive catalogs and indexes were included in the third edition and are included in this edition, also.

Although the entries in this work are not evaluated, an effort was made to describe each publication in detail, supplying enough information so that the potential user may determine whether it has any value for his or her purpose. Compilers and publishers of the catalogs and lists were asked to verify the data in the annotations and the current availability of the publications, and to add any additional information such as forthcoming revisions. This same verification process could not be followed, however, for the publications available only from the Educational Resources Information Center (ERIC); therefore, these entries were verified by checking the information in the abstracts published in *Resources in Education (RIE)*.

Three supplementary sections which appeared in the 1971 edition—professional organizations in the educational media field, periodicals in the educational media field, and media catalogs previously included but currently unavailable—are omitted from this edition for several reasons, primarily to avoid unnecessary duplication of other sources. While these sections of the GUIDE appeared to fill a need in 1971, that need no longer exists in 1977. *The Educational Media Yearbook* (R. R. Bowker Co.) lists approximately 500 media-related periodicals and includes associations in the field. The Educational Film Library Association (EFLA) publishes the *Educational Media Organizations Directory*; also, these organizations are listed in comprehensive reference tools such as the *Encyclopedia of Associations*, edited by Margaret Fisk. Periodicals in the media field are listed in the *Media Review Digest* and in the *International Index to Multimedia Information,* as well as in comprehensive periodical directories found in libraries. My decision to omit the list of out-of-print publications was based on the fact that there are only a few major catalogs and indexes which have not been revised or superseded by other publications, or entered into the ERIC system data base where they continue to be available.

I am aware of the fact that several useful lists are being published too late to be included in this revision and that others may have been omitted inadvertently. Because of a continuing interest in sources of information about educational media, suggestions and announcements concerning relevant publications will be appreciated.

Throughout the work on this publication, I have enjoyed the fullest cooperation of my colleagues at Indiana University. I am especially grateful to Martha Woolery, formerly my Administrative Assistant in the Graduate Library School, who typed the manuscript. I also wish to express my appreciation to Eva Kiewitt, Assistant Professor and Librarian of the Graduate Library School, and the former Librarian of the School of Education who was one of the original promoters and the administrator of PROBE—a computer retrieval program of the ERIC data base, developed in the Graduate Library School's Center for Research and directed by Dean Bernard Fry. This service was invaluable in identifying all of the relevant ERIC documents included for the first time in this fourth edition. I am greatly indebted as well to Beverly Teach, Assistant to the Director of Media Resources in the Audio-Visual Center, who handled the voluminous correspondence with the publishers and who gave editorial assistance and encouragement during the entire project. My indebtedness to Carolyn Guss is immeasurable; her expertise and her significant contribution to the design, organization, and compilation of the previous editions, as well as to the research study on which they were based, are reflected in every phase of this fourth edition.

MARGARET I. RUFSVOLD,
*Professor Emeritus*
Graduate Library School
Indiana University, Bloomington

# Educational Media Catalogs, Lists, Indexes, and Reviewing Services

1. **AAAS Science Film Catalog**, compiled and edited by Ann Seltz-Petrash; prepared with the assistance of the National Science Foundation. American Association for the Advancement of Science, 1776 Massachusetts Ave., N.W., Washington, DC 20036, and the R. R. Bowker Co., 1180 Avenue of the Americas, New York, NY 10036. 1975. $16.95. 398p.

> *Scope:* A comprehensive annotated list of some 5,600 films dealing with pure, applied, and social sciences and available for loan, rent, or purchase from 150 U.S. producers/distributors. The catalog is designed to meet the needs of librarians, educators, and audiovisual coordinators, in an effort to increase the use of science films and to increase the public's understanding of science. Selections were made on the basis of the producer's or distributor's descriptions, which are also the source of the annotations. The statements do not represent an endorsement or recommendation of the films' quality by either the sponsor or by the publishers. Cutoff date for inclusion of entries was September 1974. Audience levels range from primary grades through college, adult, and professional levels.
>
> *Arrangement:* In two sections, listing junior high through adult films in the first part and elementary films in the second. In each section, arrangement is by Dewey Decimal Classification number followed by titles in alphabetical order.
>
> *Entries:* Title, intended audience, running time, color or black and white,* silent or sound, free loan/rental/sales price, description of content, release date, order number, distributor code.
>
> *Special Features:* Index to subject headings; title index; producer/distributor directory.

*Hereafter b/w will be used instead of "black and white."

2. **Africa from Real to Reel: An African Filmography,** compiled by Steven Ohrn and Rebecca Riley. African Studies Association, 218 Shiffman Center, Brandeis University, Waltham, MA 02154. 1976. $10 to members; $15 to nonmembers. 144p.

> *Scope:* Approximately 1,300 16mm films on Africa distributed in the United States and Canada are described in this list. "Most of the films are of historic value only, being biased presentations shedding more light on ethnocentrism than Africa; more telling of the attraction to the strange and exotic than to the search for truth in other peoples' cultures and lives. Yet for those interested in the study of Africa, especially the history of Africa on film, this filmography should provide clues to a rich and exciting resource" (Introduction). The film descriptions are not critical; the majority were derived from printed materials supplied by producers and distributors. Grade levels are omitted because they can be misleading in many cases; however, the authors hope that the film descriptions will suggest appropriate audience levels.
>
> *Arrangement:* Alphabetical by title.
>
> *Entries:* Title, date, filmmaker/producer, color or b/w, length in minutes, geographic location, distributors in code, series note, descriptive annotation including name of consultant and of narrator, if known.
>
> *Special Features:* Distributor index; bibliography of African filmographies; photographic illustrations from some of the films.

3. **Aging: A Filmography,** by Judith Trojan. Educational Film Library Association, 43 W. Sixty-first St., New York, NY 10023. 1974. $2 prepaid. 16p.

> *Scope:* A comprehensive, critically annotated list of approximately 150 films for and about the aging individual.
>
> *Arrangement:* Alphabetical by title.
>
> *Entries:* Title or series title, length, color or b/w, date, director, producer, distributor, critical annotation, other titles if a series.
>
> *Special Features:* Introductory statement concerning the problems of the aging and their treatment in current film productions; subject index; selected features (not annotated); distributors.

4. **All Together Now: The First Complete Beatles Discography, 1961–1975,** by Harry Castleman and Walter J. Podrazik. 2d printing with corrections. Pierian Press, 5000 Washtenaw Ave., Ann Arbor, MI 48104. 1976. $14.95. 388p. (Paperback edition available from Ballantine Books)

*Scope:* Describes and lists chronologically over 460 United States and United Kingdom releases in which the Beatles have been involved as performers, writers, collaborators, backing musicians, or producers during the period June 1961 through December 1975. Recordings include those works issued both as a group member and as individual performers. Supplementary sections following the chronology provide much related information about the Beatles as a group and their individual careers.

*Arrangement:* Chronologically by date of record release, then by record label, followed by song title(s).

*Entries:* Entry number, date of release in the United States and in England, record label(s) and number(s), date(s) recorded, performers featured, producer, song titles, song writer(s), actual time of play, identification of reissued songs, identification of songs which have not appeared in LP records.

*Special Features:* Album/song title index; musical influences on the Beatles; bootleg recordings; Beatle-related records by other performers, Beatle recording myths; complete list of Apple singles and albums, and Dark Horse and Ring O' records; motion picture appearances; books by and about the Beatles; complete list of gold records; 15 years of the weekly position charts from *Melody Maker* and *Billboard*; almost 100 photographic illustrations primarily from recording "sleeves."

5. **Alternatives: A Filmography,** compiled by Nadine Covert and Esmé Dick, assisted by Carol A. Emmens. Educational Film Library Association, 43 W. Sixty-first St., New York, NY 10023. 1974. $2. 12p.

*Scope:* A selected list of titles prepared in connection with a workshop held at Mills College, Oakland, California, in February 1974, at which alternatives in education and lifestyles were explored through films. With only a few exceptions, the titles included were screened by both editors and the annotations were written in collaboration. Subjects include: arts and crafts, city planning, consumerism, education—day care, education—free schools open classrooms, education—urban school problems, health and medicine, lifestyles—general, lifestyles—communes, lifestyles—women, politics, religion.

*Arrangement:* Alphabetical by title.

*Entries:* Title, length, color or b/w, date, director, producer/distributor, descriptive/critical annotation.

*Special Features:* Distributors' names and addresses; brief selected bibliography; subject index; Alternative Film Workshop Participants (enclosed list).

6. **American Film Festival Guide.** Educational Film Library Association, 43 W. Sixty-first St., New York, NY 10023. Annual. 1959–66 issues, $1 each; 1967, unavailable; 1968–72 issues, $2 each; 1973 to date, $2.50 each. *Cumulative Index* 1959–63. 50¢. 16p. Payment must accompany orders under $50.

> *Scope:* Descriptions of the films shown at the annual EFLA American Film Festival. "The purpose is to showcase outstanding 16mm films of the preceding year—films which will be of interest for programming in schools, universities, libraries, museums, churches, and for other community uses. The Festival covers the full range of 16mm nontheatrical film production: documentaries on current issues, cultural films, children's films, curriculum films, health films, industrial and business films, experimental films" (*EFLA 1975*, p. 4). All films are preselected for showing at the festivals by local subject-category preview committees.
>
> *Arrangement:* By approximately 40 broad subject categories, then alphabetical by title.
>
> *Entries:* Title, color or b/w, running time, purchase/rental price, producer, director, distributor. Brief annotation gives statement of the purpose, recommended audience, and a description of the content.
>
> *Special Features:* Title index; distributor directory; advertiser index; out-of-competition screenings.

7. **American Film Review: Films of America.** v.15. The American Educational and Historical Film Center, Eastern College, St. Davids, PA 19087. 1976. Free. 31p.

> *Scope:* Motion pictures endorsed and approved by the American Educational and Historical Film Center; selected by "a distinguished committee of evaluators who personally reviewed the films not only for technical skills, but also for accuracy of content and freedom from subversive bias" (Introduction). The films fall into five broad categories of history: American citizenship, American free enterprise, American heroes, American landmarks, America and the Communist challenge. More than 100 titles.
>
> *Arrangement:* Alphabetical by title under broad categories. No index. Table of contents by broad categories.
>
> *Entries:* Title, producer, distributor, color or b/w, running time, audience by grade level. Descriptive annotation of 10–25 words in 1–3 sentences, with specific content notes where necessary.
>
> *Special Features:* Directory of film producers and distributors; trustees and officers of the Center; members of the film selection committee.

8. **American Folklore Films & Videotapes: An Index.** Center for Southern Folklore, P.O. Box 4081, 1216 Peabody Ave., Memphis, TN 38104. 1976. $15. 338p. (Updated supplement in preparation in 1976)

*Scope:* This reference work is a comprehensive listing of more than 1,800 films and videotapes on American folk traditions. In addition to the alphabetical list of titles available for distribution, there is a section on special collections—scarce noncirculating films, videotapes, and film footage, arranged by location. The index is illustrated with 170 rare old stills and reproductions.
*Arrangement:* Alphabetical by title.
*Entries:* Title, running time, format, color or b/w, date of release or production, distributors, brief description including pertinent data on the filmmaker.
*Special Features:* Subject index with numerous cross references; photographic illustrations; distributors' title listings; distributors' addresses.

9. **American Issues Forum Film List,** compiled by the Educational Film Library Association, 43 W. Sixty-first St., New York, NY 10023. 1975. $1 prepaid. 32p.

*Scope:* A selected annotated list of 200 films compiled by the EFLA staff and consultants in support of the American Issues Forum, a Bicentennial program developed around 9 monthly issues and subtopics: A Nation of Nations; The Land of Plenty; Certain Unalienable Rights; A More Perfect Union—the American Government; Working in America; The Business of America; America in the World; Growing Up in America; Life, Liberty, and the Pursuit of Happiness.
*Arrangement:* By 9 topics and 36 subtopics, then alphabetical by title.
*Entries:* Title, length, color or b/w, date, director, producer, distributor, descriptive/evaluative annotation, initials of evaluator.
*Special Features:* Note to film programmers; bibliography; directory of distributors; title index.

10. **An Annotated and Classified List of 16mm Films on Urban Studies: New Towns, Urban Problems, City and Regional Planning,** by Irving Lewis Allen. Council of Planning Librarians, P.O. Box 229, Monticello, IL 61856. 1975. $3. 31p. Available also in microfiche only from ERIC Document Reproduction Service, P.O. Box 190, Arlington, VA 22210. Apply for current price. ED 115 537. (Exchange Bibliography no.838)

*Scope:* A selected annotated list of approximately 100 16mm films on urban studies produced, for the most part, after 1960, and culled from such sources as the film bibliography periodically issued by the U.S. Department of Housing and Urban Development, film reviews in the *Journal of the American Institute of Planners,* commercial producer's and distributor's catalogs, university film library catalogs, other bibliographies, and direct-mail advertisements. The annotations are descriptive and are culled from these sources. The author deliberately selected films that "seem to have some social science content" and omitted "films that deal primarily with physical planning and design and with certain urban problems, such as transportation" (Compiler's Note). The list includes films about British and Canadian cities and a few about cities elsewhere in the world; all are in English.

*Arrangement:* By subject category, then alphabetical by title.

*Entries:* Title or series title, description of content, producer, distributor and address, color or b/w, free loan/rental, length, date.

11. **Annotated Bibliography of Commercially Produced Audio, Printed, and Visual Career Education Materials,** by Robert W. Sackrison and LeVene A. Olson. Department of Occupational, Adult, and Safety Education, Marshall University, Huntington, WV 25701. Available in microfiche and hard copy from ERIC Document Reproduction Service, P.O. Box 190, Arlington, VA 22210. 1975. Apply for current prices. 35p. ED 109 430.

*Scope:* A representative sample of commercially produced materials in the areas of career awareness, career orientation, and career exploration—ranging in level from kindergarten to adult age groups. Included are multimedia materials, 16mm films, 8mm filmloops, filmstrips, slides, records and cassettes, and printed materials. "An effort was made to delete materials which would appear dated to the user" (Abstract, p.1). Inclusion in this bibliography does not mean an endorsement or approval of any product or manufacturer.

*Arrangement:* By age group, then by type of medium.

*Entries:* Code indicating subject, grade level, producer/distributor in code, title of series or set, descriptive annotation, objectives, types of hardware and software, length in minutes/number of items, color or b/w, sound or silent, individual titles in set or series.

*Special Features:* Codes, names, and addresses of producers/distributors.

12. **An Annotated Bibliography of Instructional Materials which Emphasize Positive Work Ethics,** by Charles Curry. Program of Agricultural Education, College of Education, Virginia Polytechnic Institute and State University, Blacksburg, VA 24061, in cooperation with the Division of Vocational Education, State Department of Education, Rich-

mond, VA 23216. Available in microfiche and hard copy from ERIC Document Reproduction Service, P.O. Box 190, Arlington, VA 22210. 1975. Apply for current prices. 122p. ED 115 766.

*Scope:* A list of 56 printed and audiovisual titles which were evaluated and selected from a total of 140 items solicited from vocational teacher education departments, curriculum development centers, research coordinating units, representatives of the National Network for Curriculum Coordination in Vocational Education, state departments of education, and other vocational education agencies. The author's intent was to include only those materials which deal specifically with developing pride in good workmanship, job attainment and holding power, occupational decision making, self-image, ethical conduct, career advancement, reasons for working, and potential job satisfaction. Each abstract was written and signed by the person from the agency which submitted the material for review.

*Arrangement:* Alphabetical by title.

*Entries:* Title, date, name of developer, subject, type of medium, length in minutes/pages, color or b/w, intended audience, target level of audience for professional use, specialized training requirements, ordering information, descriptive abstract, agency address and name of person submitting abstract, date of abstract.

*Special Features:* Photograph of each item; index of agencies by state. Each entry is a one-page copy of the questionnaire on which the data and the abstract are recorded.

13. **An Annotated Catalog of Visual Materials Relating to the Identification and Management of Handicapping Conditions of Preschool Children,** compiled by Del Lawhon and Linda Thornton. Appalachia Educational Laboratory, Charleston, WV 25301. Available in microfiche and hard copy from ERIC Document Reproduction Service, P.O. Box 190, Arlington, VA 22210. 1975. Apply for current prices. 168p. ED 112 605.

*Scope:* A list of 232 films, filmstrips, slides, transparencies, and videotapes which were culled from catalogs and from the informational brochures of producers and distributors. Divided into two parts, the first section of the catalog describes and evaluates 118 titles concerned with the following subjects: autism, Down's syndrome, emotionally disturbed, hearing impaired, informational, instructional, language, learning disorders, mental retardation, physical and neurologically handicapped, visually impaired, testing and assessment. The second section lists the titles which were not reviewed.

*Arrangement:* First section—alphabetical by title; second section—by type of medium.

*Entries:* Title, type of medium, length, producer, distributor, sale and rental prices, summary and critical comment (first section entries), audience level, additional sources.

*Special Features:* Indexes to visuals reviewed and recommended, first by title, then by subject; visual information form (for updating the catalog).

14. **Annotated Film Bibliography: Child Development and Early Childhood Education,** compiled by Carol Lou Holt. Child Day Care Association, 915 Olive St., St. Louis, MO 63101. 1973. $3.40 postpaid. 148p. Available also in microfiche and hard copy from ERIC Document Reproduction Service, P.O. Box 190, Arlington, VA 22210. Apply for current prices. ED 093 496.

*Scope:* A classified and annotated list of 16mm films for teacher training, parent education, and children compiled from a variety of sources including the film showings for the past several years at the conferences of the National Association for the Education of Young Children, recent Head Start film lists, the 1970 White House Conference on Children film list, and film distributor's advertisements. The films are not evaluated.

*Arrangement:* Alphabetical by title, with a subject index.

*Entries:* Title, color or b/w, length, producer/distributor, descriptive annotation, date and rental/purchase prices for some titles.

*Special Features:* Names and addresses of film sources.

15. **Annotated List of Audio-Visual Materials with Sexual Content,** compiled by Martha Harsanyi. Institute for Sex Research, 416 Morrison Hall, Indiana University, Bloomington, IN 47401. 1975. $1. 28p.

*Scope:* A list of films, slides, and videotapes selected "as possible audiovisual support for a college level (or above) human sexuality curriculum" (p.1). Many of the titles are shown at the Institute's summer program. The annotations include critical evaluations; however, the introduction points out that, inasmuch as the needs and uses of educators and therapists vary considerably, the annotations should not be taken as final judgment but rather as a general aid and starting point in the user's selection process.

*Arrangement:* By subject categories.

*Entries:* Title, running time, type of medium, color or b/w, sound or silent, descriptive and evaluative annotation, distributor, rental and purchase prices.

*Special Features:* Brief list of bibliographies and catalogs; addresses of distributors.

16. **Annotated Listing of Films: Physical Education and Recreation for Impaired, Disabled, and Handicapped Persons.** 2d ed. Physical Education and Recreation for the Handicapped: Information and Research Utilization Center, American Alliance for Health, Physical Education, and Recreation, 1201 Sixteenth St., N.W., Washington, DC 20036. 1976. Free. 118p. (An updated and expanded edition of the 1973 publication of the same title)

*Scope:* A list of 314 films considered to be appropriate, interesting, educational, and useful for professional persons who deal with impaired, disabled, and handicapped persons, physical educators in general, adapted physical education specialists, community and therapeutic recreation personnel, general and special educators, volunteers, parents, and the general public. Many films are considered appropriate for viewing by classes in medicine, nursing, psychology, social work, and by clergymen. Several related and ancillary areas have been added to this edition, e.g., media presentations about specific handicapping conditions, driver education, transportation and mobility concerns. Relevant media not specifically designed for persons who work with the handicapped are again included. "Films marked with an asterisk are not specifically for or with individuals having any identifiable handicapping condition. Those marked with two asterisks have been designed for and/or can be used with participants themselves" (Introduction). Every entry in the guide was previewed and evaluated by at least one member of the Center's staff. The list is in two parts, with the first 123 titles taken verbatim from the 1973 edition and an additional 191 new titles listed in the second part.

*Arrangement:* Alphabetical by title in each part.

*Entries:* Entry number, title or series title followed by individual titles, size (mm), sound or silent, color or b/w, length, distributor and address, purchase/rental price for some entries, detailed description of content.

*Special Features:* Publications and sources for audiovisual materials; subject index.

17. **Annual Index to Popular Music Record Reviews,** by Andrew W. Armitage and Dean Tudor. Scarecrow Press, Inc., Box 656, Metuchen, NJ 08840. Volume 1972, published in 1973. $13.50. 467p.; Volume 1973, published in 1974. $20. 681p.; Volume 1974, published in 1976. $20. 597p. Volume 1975, published in 1976. $20. 552p.

*Scope:* The latest volume (1975 reviews) includes citations to individual long-playing records and reviews which appeared in 60 periodicals. The following 13 categories of popular music are included: rock, mood (pop), country, old-time bluegrass, folk, ethnic, jazz, blues, rhythm and blues, popular religious music, stage and film, band, humor. The index can be used to locate a particular review and/or as a record selection tool based upon the evaluations cited.

*Arrangement:* By categories in the order listed above, then alphabetical by artist or by anthology title.

*Entries:* Number, artist, album title, label and serial number, number of discs per set, reel-to-reel serial number and price, 4-track cartridge serial number and price, 8-track cassette serial number and price, country of origin if not the United States, reissued release, periodical title, month or number of issue, page citation, number of words in review, reviewer's evaluation: 0(poor) to 5a(superb) recording.

*Special Features:* Periodicals indexed; Directory of Record Labels; Specialty Record Stores; Artist Index; Anthology and Concerts Index.

18. **AOA Catalog of Films on Aging.** Administration on Aging, Social and Rehabilitation Service, U.S. Department of Health, Education, and Welfare. Available from the Superintendent of Documents, U.S. Government Printing Office, Washington, DC 20402. 1973. 60¢. 59p.

*Scope:* An annotated list of 121 films, 8 filmstrips, 17 slide sets, 9 plays, and 4 state television series of interest in the broad field of aging and currently available from government and nongovernment sources. Subjects include: health care, nutrition, safety, health rehabilitation, income, living arrangements, retirement preparation, retirement roles and activities.

*Arrangement:* Divided by type of medium; film section lists titles alphabetically under broad subject headings; remaining sections list titles alphabetically under type of medium.

*Entries:* Title or series title, description of content, type of medium and size (mm), color or b/w, sound or silent with script, length in minutes/number of slides, date, producer, available on free loan or rental price, purchase price, name and address of distributor.

*Special Features:* Title index.

19. **Arizona in . . . 16mm Films, 8mm Films, Filmloops, Filmstrips, Slides, Transparencies, Cassettes, Records, Photos, Prints, Posters, Charts, Study Prints, Maps, Flags, Book Returns, Bookmarks, Foods, Micro-**

**film, Place Mats, Relief Model Kits, Stereo Picture Reels,** compiled by Mary Choncoff. Libraries/Learning Resources, Arizona Department of Education, Phoenix, AZ 85007. Available in microfiche and hard copy from ERIC Document Reproduction Service, P.O. Box 190, Arlington, VA 22210. 1976. Apply for current prices. 90p. ED 119 938.

*Scope:* A compilation of both instructional and promotional nonprint media which is the product of a year's search through numerous selection aids, catalogs, conference exhibits, bookstores, and shops at Arizona historical sites. The materials deal with a variety of subjects including Arizona American Indian peoples and cultures, Arizona geographical and geological phenomena (the Grand Canyon, the desert, the petrified forest), and various Arizona-related historical and biographical data. Most of the materials were produced during the 1960s and 1970s.

*Arrangement:* By categories of materials in the order mentioned in the title, then alphabetical by title.

*Entries:* Title or series title, producer, date if available, length in minutes/frames/items, sound or silent, color or b/w, description, individual titles if a series, source abbreviation, price if available.

*Special Features:* Source directories for 16mm films, for 8mm films and filmloops, for filmstrips, for cassettes, for records, and for Arizona flags.

20. **Audiovisual Materials for Teaching Economics,** prepared by the Audiovisual Materials Evaluation Committee, Sidney J. Kronish, Chairman, for the Joint Council on Economic Education, 1212 Avenue of the Americas, New York, NY 10036. 1972. $2; $1.60 each for 10 or more copies. 55p. (Supersedes *Study Materials for Economic Education in the Schools, 1969*)

*Scope:* A report and catalog of evaluated materials designed to help elementary and secondary school teachers in their selection of economic education audiovisual media and to indicate to producers, through a statistical analysis, those subject areas in need of new materials. For example, the findings reveal that instructional aids for the elementary grades are very scarce, as are materials on the problems of developing nations. All materials submitted were evaluated by at least three members of the committee using criteria of economic analysis, objectivity, and effectiveness. The introduction states that "only those items which add to the students' usable store of concepts, generalizations, and theories" are recommended; purely descriptive materials are not included. Subject categories are: general nature of economics, income determination and growth, role of government and economic institutions, international economics, comparative systems and economic history.

*Arrangement:* By subject categories, then alphabetical by title.

*Entries:* Title, type of medium, length, color or b/w, sound or silent, producer/distributor, date, subject headings, grade level, analytical concepts and generalizations, descriptive annotation.

*Special Features:* Introduction which includes purpose, criteria, committee members, evaluation process, statistical analysis, and state of the art; listing of materials by grade level; title index; list of producers and distributors.

21. **Audio-Visual Materials for Teaching Library Science: An Evaluation of One Hundred Selected Titles Produced from 1968–1973,** by Myron Jack May. Department of Library Science, Ball State University, Muncie, IN 47906. Available in microfiche and hard copy from ERIC Document Reproduction Service, P.O. Box 190, Arlington, VA 22210. 1974. Apply for current prices. 54p. ED 100 315.

*Scope:* This evaluative bibliography of commercially produced materials for library education and instruction in the use of libraries includes films, filmstrips, kits, phonodiscs, tapes, cassettes, and charts. Each title is accompanied by a review from one of several reviewing services such as EFLA, *Booklist, Previews,* Landers, and others; audience levels are suggested.

*Arrangement:* Alphabetical by title.

*Entries:* Title, type of medium, production date, length, speed, color or b/w, sound or silent, audience or grade level, producer, distributor, an evaluative annotation, Library of Congress catalog card number, source of review.

*Special Features:* Analytical indexes for: children's literature, history, libraries in general, library administration, library use skills, motion picture production, other media production, media selection and use, reference and research. Lists of distributors and review sources.

22. **Audiovisual Materials for the Teaching of Language Acquisition: An Annotated Bibliography,** by Rosemary Tripp and Sophia Behrens. ERIC Clearinghouse on Languages and Linguistics, Center for Applied Linguistics, Arlington, VA 22209. Available in microfiche and hard copy from ERIC Document Reproduction Service, P.O. Box 190, Arlington, VA 22210. 1976. Apply for current prices. 13p. ED 116 496. (CAL-ERIC/CLL Series on Languages and Linguistics, no.32)

*Scope:* An annotated list of films, audiocassettes and videotapes on such subjects as children's acquisition of morphology, phonology, and semantics; vocabulary and language development; the acquisition of specific items such as negatives and passives; and abnormal speech acquisition. The annotations are descriptive, not evaluative; wherever possible the appropriate audience is suggested. The list represents "a sampling of all audiovisual aids in language teaching" (Introduction).

*Arrangement:* Alphabetical by title or series title.

*Entries:* Title or series title, date if available, running time, description of content, grade level, distributor, rental/purchase prices (1976).

*Special Features:* Source addresses.

23. **Audiovisual Materials for the Teaching of Language Variation: An Annotated Bibliography,** by Rosemary Tripp and Sophia Behrens. ERIC Clearinghouse on Languages and Linguistics, Center for Applied Linguistics, Arlington, VA 22209. Available in microfiche and hard copy from ERIC Document Reproduction Service, P.O. Box 190, Arlington, VA 22210. 1976. Apply for current prices. 12p. ED 116 495. (CAL-ERIC/CLL Series on Languages and Linguistics, no.31)

*Scope:* "The materials presented here are a sampling of all audiovisual aids in language teaching" (Introduction). Included are LP recordings, cassettes, and 16mm films on such topics as regional dialect studies, language change, language acquisition, social dialects, and language in education. The annotations are descriptive, not evaluative; wherever possible the appropriate audience is suggested.

*Arrangement:* Alphabetical by title or series title.

*Entries:* Title or series title, date if available, running time, description of content, grade level, distributor, rental/purchase prices (1976).

*Special Features:* Source addresses.

24. **Audiovisual Materials in Dental Education 1973.** Education Development Branch, Division of Dental Health, Bureau of Health Resources Development, Health Resources Administration, Public Health Service, U.S. Department of Health, Education, and Welfare, Bethesda, MD 20014. 1973. Free. 318p. (DHEW Publication no.HRA 74–24)

*Scope:* A comprehensive annotated list of 1,495 titles of films, filmstrips, slide sets, and programmed texts, compiled from the data obtained by the Office of Educational Resources and Studies, American Association of Dental Schools, through its National Survey of Audiovisual Media. The listing includes only those materials currently available at the time of the survey and only those reported as used by educators who participated in the survey and some additional titles submitted by commercial distributors. Subjects in addition to dentistry include: anatomy, inservice education, medicine, microbiology, pathology (general), pharmacology, physiology, and psychology. None of the materials listed has been evaluated.

*Arrangement:* Alphabetical by title.

*Entries:* Title, producer, date, type of medium, color or b/w, sound or silent, length in minutes/slides/frames, distributor(s), descriptive annotation.

*Special Features:* Index of titles by subject areas; names and addresses of distributors.

25. **Audio-Visual Resource Guide.** 9th ed. Available from Friendship Press, National Council of Churches, 475 Riverside Dr., New York, NY 10027. 1973. $8.95. 477p. (Supplement scheduled for publication in 1978)

*Scope:* More than 2,500 films, filmstrips, discs, tapes, slides, and a few graphic materials dealing with these subjects: God, Jesus, Bible, the Church, history, the individual, health, the family, the community and nation, world community, national/international critical issues, science and technology, arts and leisure, education. Many titles in the *Guide* are secular in application.

*Arrangement:* Alphabetical by title.

*Entries:* Title, type of medium, length, color or b/w if film or filmstrip, size and speed if disc or tape, guide if available, producer, date of production, distributor, sale and/or rental rate, 75–200-word description of content, 75–200-word evaluation critique, recommendation (highly recommended, recommended, acceptable, limited, on the basis of evaluations prepared by leaders in Christian education meetings in 50 interdenominational committees throughout the United States), principal teaching purpose, recommended audience, subject heading codes referring to the specific subject heading(s) under which the unit is listed in the subject heading index.

*Special Features:* Subject-heading index with titles listed alphabetically; distributor index; list of selected feature-length films available in 16mm; brief bibliography of books and periodicals related to media resources.

26. **Audiovisual Resources for Instructional Development,** compiled by Thomas Wilds and others. The Council for Exceptional Children, 1920 Association Dr., Reston, VA 22091. 1975. $6. 256p. (CEC Information Services Program)

*Scope:* Designed to assist persons providing services to the handicapped, including parents, educators, rehabilitation personnel, administrators, and counselors. Included are more than 1,000 titles of cassettes and tapes, filmloops, films, filmstrips, multimedia kits, slide shows, transparencies, and videotapes selected from distributors' catalogs and other lists on the basis of the following criteria: the material must be current, must be available, must be of audiovisual nature, and must present techniques, models, or other specific information that can aid in providing services to the handicapped.

*Arrangement:* By type of medium, then alphabetical by title.

*Entries:* Title or series title, descriptive annotation, individual titles if a series, producer, distributor, sale and rental prices, color or b/w, type of medium, length in minutes/number of frames or items, Library of Congress catalog card number if available.

*Special Features:* Subject index; Distributors' Guide.

27. **Audio-Visual Resources in Population Education and Family Planning: An International Guide for Social Work Educators.** International Association of Schools of Social Work, 345 E. Forty-Sixth St., New York, NY 10017. 1976. $2. 148p.

*Scope:* Includes over 200 annotated titles of films, filmstrips, slides, and tapes. A separate section contains a discussion of audiovisual methods and equipment.

*Arrangement:* Alphabetical by title.

*Entries:* Title, date, color or b/w, length in minutes/number of frames or slides, producer/distributor, description of content.

*Special Features:* Names of sources for audiovisual materials in population education and distributors of audiovisual equipment; selected bibliography; index.

28. **Audiovisuals for Nutrition Education: Selected Evaluative Reviews from the Journal of Nutrition Education,** compiled by Sue Ellen Rowe. Society for Nutrition Education, 2140 Shattuck Ave., Suite 1110, Berkeley, CA 94704. 1975. $2 to members; $2.50 to nonmembers. 28p. (National Nutrition Education Clearing House, Nutrition Education Resource Series, no.9)

*Scope:* Critical reviews of more than 170 titles within 121 numerical entries of nonprint materials. Categories of media included are coloring books, flannelboard stories, games and kits; audiotapes and records; charts, posters and study prints; films and videotapes; filmstrips, slides, and transparencies.

*Arrangement:* Alphabetical by title within media categories.

*Entries:* Entry number, type of medium, audience levels, title, producer, date if available, source with address, format, sound or silent, color or b/w, length in minutes/frames/items, accompanying materials if any, rental/purchase price, review.

*Special Features:* Author/publisher/producer index; subject index; title index.

29. **Auditory Learning Materials for Special Education: Catalog,** by Marsha Smith and Phyllis O'Connor, in conjunction with the Consortium on Auditory Learning Materials for the Handicapped, Regional Instructional Materials Center for Handicapped Children and Youth, Michigan State University, East Lansing, MI 48823. Available in microfiche and hard copy from ERIC Document Reproduction Service, P.O. Box 190, Arlington, VA 22210. 1974. Apply for current prices. 152p. ED 102 757.

*Scope:* There are approximately 100 titles of cassettes, phonodiscs, filmstrips, transparencies, booklets, manuals, and teacher's guides in this list; a majority are cassettes accompanied by filmstrips, and each of the materials was examined "firsthand" by a member of the staff. The opening section of the catalog describes procedures used to evaluate and classify the materials and includes a list of descriptors, sample forms, and an explanation of the learner classification system. Broad subjects of auditory materials included are: affective domain, career development, communication skills, health and safety, mathematics, music, science, and social studies.

*Arrangement:* Alphabetical by title.

*Entries:* Title, picture of the item and a one-paragraph description, author, producer and address, date, price, student objectives, information on content and procedures, equipment needed, subject area, grade level.

*Special Features:* Indexes of titles, producers, broad subject areas, and recommended interest and/or use levels; accompanying cassette tape and brochure presenting practical suggestions for designing auditory instruction and for making auditory instruction meaningful.

30. **Available Recordings of American Poetry and Poets,** compiled by Homer E. Salley. University of Toledo, Toledo, OH 43606. Available in microfiche and hard copy from ERIC Document Reproduction Service, P.O. Box 190, Arlington, VA 22210. 1975. 48p. Apply for current prices. ED 114 059.

*Scope:* A list of phonodiscs and tape cassettes of American poetry and poets available from commercial sources and from the Library of

Congress Recording Laboratory and the National Council of Teachers of English. The list is analytical—all works of one poet are listed under his or her name, including works that are only part of a collection of several poets' works. Entries are not annotated.

*Arrangement:* Alphabetical by poet.

*Entries:* Record title, list of poems on the record, number of records in the set, label and label number.

*Special Features:* Record publishing companies with addresses.

31. **AVLINE (Audiovisuals On-Line).** The National Library of Medicine in cooperation with the Association of American Medical Colleges provides information on selected health science materials to *MED-LINE* subscribers (Medical Literature Analysis and Retrieval System On-Line) at more than 300 institutions, government agencies, and companies. Further information about AVLINE and the Educational Materials Project is available from the National Library of Medicine, 8600 Rockville Pike, Bethesda, MD 20014, and the Association of American Medical Colleges, Division of Educational Resources and Programs, One Dupont Circle, N.W., Washington, DC 20036.

*Scope:* An on-line data base from which teachers, students, librarians, researchers, and practitioners may retrieve references to appraised educational materials in the health sciences for national distribution. This cooperative project became operational in 1976 making possible identification of the materials that were appraised by subject matter specialists selected by the AAMC. Materials also are assessed for instructional design, content validity, and technical quality. Items receiving an overall rating of "recommended" are processed for entry into the AVLINE system and are cataloged according to the Anglo-American Cataloging Rules for nonprint media. AVLINE may be searched by several descriptors including: subject, title, media, audience level, and availability. There is an abstract for each material. Citations may be printed on-line at the user's terminal or off-line and mailed to the user from the computer center.

*Arrangement:* Optional at user's request.

*Special Features:* (searchable fields): Main heading; subheading; title; where and how item may be obtained; name of principal author/producer; intended audience; review date; series; procurement source; year of production; language; media; educational design; text words.

32. **A Bibliography of Affective Materials for the Adolescent Years,** by Jackie Bolen. California Learning Resource Center, 600 S. Common-

wealth Ave., Suite 1304, Los Angeles, CA 90005. Available in microfiche and hard copy from ERIC Document Reproduction Service, P.O. Box 190, Arlington, VA 22210. 1973. Apply for current prices. 71p. ED 078 617.

*Scope:* An annotated bibliography of 146 instructional materials judged to be useful to teachers who deal with normal and abnormal adolescent affective behavior in junior and senior high schools. Included are 73 filmstrips with recordings or guides, 40 16mm and 8mm films, 2 transparencies, 1 simulation, 3 recordings, 24 books and booklets, and 3 miscellaneous items. Some of the subjects represented are teen-parent relationships, sex education, alcoholism, running away, cheating, maturation and growth, Afro-American history, American Indian studies.

*Arrangement:* By type of medium, then by publisher/producer number.

*Entries:* Publisher/producer code number, title or album title, series title, author, length in minutes/number of items/pages/frames, description of content, individual titles if a series, color or b/w, purchase or rental price, dates for some printed materials.

*Special Features:* Topic areas index; list of 21 publishers/producers with addresses.

33. **Bibliography of Audiovisual Instructional Materials for the Teaching of Spanish: Kindergarten through Grade Twelve.** Available from Bureau of Compensatory Education Evaluation and Research, California State Department of Education, P.O. Box 271, Sacramento, CA 95802. 1976. 75¢. 129p. Available also in microfiche only from ERIC Document Reproduction Service, P.O. Box 190, Arlington, VA 22210. Apply for current prices. ED 119 508.

*Scope:* The work of the members of a statewide committee who previewed and evaluated the materials, this bibliography supplements two previously published lists of printed materials on the same subject. Included are films, filmstrips, games, puzzles, multimedia kits, records, tapes, slides, posters, charts, and photographs. Many materials, especially those related to very controversial subjects, were reviewed but not included. The entries are organized into 17 subject categories: art, bilingual education, career education, culture, driver education, games and puzzles, guidance, health, language arts, literature, mathematics, music, physical education, science, social science, supplementary materials, and vocational education.

*Arrangement:* By subject categories in the order listed above, then alphabetical by title or series title.

*Entries:* Title or series title, type of medium, publisher/distributor, date, price, color or b/w, sound or silent, length, grade level, appropriate uses, English or Spanish sound track, descriptive annotation.

*Special Features:* Members of the Spanish Bibliography Committee; tabular index to types of materials by title; directory of distributors, publishers, and manufacturers.

34. **Bibliography of Instructional Materials for the Teaching of German: Kindergarten through Grade Twelve,** compiled by John Dusel and others, California State Department of Education, Sacramento, CA 95814. Available in microfiche and hard copy from ERIC Document Reproduction Service, P.O. Box 190, Arlington, VA 22210. 1975. Apply for current prices. 85p. ED 112 661.

*Scope:* A selected list of texts, charts, pamphlets, posters, periodicals, readers, filmstrips, films, records, and slides which were previewed and evaluated by the German Bibliography Committee. Materials were eliminated if they were of poor quality, culturally inaccurate, or out-of-date. The entries are divided into seven subject categories: art, language arts, literature, music, science-mathematics, social sciences, and other materials.

*Arrangement:* By categories in the order listed above, then alphabetical by title.

*Entries:* Subject abbreviation, title, type of material abbreviation, author (print) series title, publisher/distributor, date, length in pages/minutes/items, color or b/w, abbreviation for language interest level and for maturity level (age/grade), description of content.

*Special Features:* Index to titles by series; directory of distributors and publishers; tabular index to types of materials by title; members of the German Bibliography Committee.

35. **Bibliography of Nonprint Instructional Materials on the American Indian,** prepared by the Instructional Development Program for the Institute of Indian Services and Research, Brigham Young University, Provo, UT 84601. 1972. $2.95. 221p.

*Scope:* A comprehensive bibliography of 16mm films, 8mm filmloops, filmstrips, 35mm slides, transparencies, study prints, maps, charts, recordings, and multimedia kits concerning all aspects of the life and culture of Indians of North America and South America. The information was gathered from a variety of sources and from correspondence with producers; the resulting list was checked against the various media indexes and directories.

*Arrangement:* Alphabetical by title.

*Entries:* Title, type of medium, length (minutes, number of frames/
slides/pieces), sound or silent, color or b/w, producer/distributor,
date when available, grade level, series, descriptive annotation,
subject heading(s).

*Special Features:* List of subject headings; subject index; distributors'
names and addresses.

36. **Bilingual Audiovisual Materials.** Bilingual Resource Center, New
York City Board of Education, Brooklyn, NY 11201 (Dissemination
Kit: K-8DS). Available in microfiche and hard copy from ERIC Docu-
ment Reproduction Service, P.O. Box 190, Arlington, VA 22210. 1973.
Apply for current prices. 33p. ED 084 919.

*Scope:* An annotated list of films, filmstrips, records, cassettes, tapes,
texts with records/tapes, and other media related to bilingual
teaching methods. The materials range in level from primary grades
through high school and are available from a number of different
producers/distributors including the Center.

*Arrangement:* Alphabetical by subject under type of medium, then
alphabetical by title.

*Entries:* Title, length in number of items/reels/minutes, color or b/w,
producer/publisher/distributor, language, date, description of content, grade level.

37. **Bilingual Bicultural Materials: A Listing for Library Resource Centers.** Model Bilingual Bicultural Learning Resource Center, El Paso
Public Schools, 107 N. Collingsworth Ave., El Paso, TX 79905. Available in microfiche and hard cover from ERIC Document Reproduction Service, P.O. Box 190, Arlington, VA 22210. 1974. Apply for current prices. 76p. ED 098 975.

*Scope:* This list is the result of a materials evaluation project carried
on by 11 teams of elementary school teachers and librarians in the
El Paso school system. Each item included was used by teachers in
more than one school. Recommendations are made for first, second,
or third purchase, or in some cases, titles are designated "not appropriate" or "not recommended." Included are 216 kits, 21 sound
filmstrips, 43 records, 253 books, and 43 other items such as slides,
transparencies, games, and models.

*Arrangement:* By type of medium, then alphabetical by title.

*Entries:* Title, producer code, date, type of medium, contents, source,
suggested Dewey Decimal Classification number, grade level, recommendation.

*Special Features:* Key to abbreviations; sources used; sample form
used by evaluators; teachers and librarians who served on evaluation teams.

38. **The Birds and the Beasts Were There: Animals in Their Natural Habitats; a Multimedia Bibliography Revised,** by Marjorie Sullivan and Helen Strader. School of Library Science, Emporia Kansas State College, for the Kansas Association of School Librarians. Available in microfiche and hard copy from ERIC Document Reproduction Service, P.O. Box 190, Arlington, VA 22210. 1973. Apply for current prices. 35p. ED 079 947.

> *Scope:* This annotated list of 247 print and nonprint media dealing with ecology and animal life is designed to assist school personnel in selecting materials suitable for pupils in grades 4 through 6 and 9 through 12. The elementary school collection consists of 65 books, 43 16mm films, 33 recordings and slides, and 8 periodicals. The secondary school collection includes 80 books and 26 "other media." Selection of materials is based upon their "appeal to youngsters" and "qualities of text and format contributing to their value" (p.1). Reference works are excluded.
>
> *Arrangement:* In 2 sections: elementary grades 4-6, and secondary grades 9-12; then by type of medium, with books listed alphabetically by author and with nonbook media and periodicals listed alphabetically by title.
>
> *Entries:* Author (books), title, series title, publisher/producer, date, length in pages/minutes/number of discs/frames/slides, size, sound or silent, color or b/w, brief descriptive annotation.
>
> *Special Features:* Bibliographies of Sources; materials for teaching; distributors of nonprint media.

39. **The Black Record: A Selective Discography of Afro-Americana on Audio Discs,** by Bernice Dain and David Nevin. Rev. ed. Audio/Visual Department, John M. Olin Library, Washington University, St. Louis, MO 63130. Available in microfiche and hard copy from ERIC Document Reproduction Service, P.O. Box 190, Arlington, VA 22210. 1973. Apply for current prices. 19p. ED 094 081. (Library Studies no.11)

> *Scope:* More than 250 phonodiscs dealing with black history. Documentary and spoken word recording classifications include biographical material, speeches, poetry, prose, and drama. Includes such persons as W. E. B. Du Bois, Frederick Douglass, Booker T. Washington, Malcolm X, Martin Luther King, Jr., and Stokely Carmichael. Folk music classifications include rhythm and blues, game songs, ballads, hollers and shouts, spirituals and gospel songs, work songs and calls. Emphasis is placed on "authentic" folk recordings which range from origins in Africa to "Songs of the Selma-Montgomery March."

*Arrangement:* Divided into 4 sections—documentary and spoken word; folk music, African origins; folk music, new world roots and growth; soundtracks and musicals.

*Entries:* Local call number, title and author/artist or author/artist and title, 10–15-word description of content or list of contributors, producer/phonorecord number.

*Author's Note:* All the recordings in this listing are in the John M. Olin Library, Washington University, which has been conscientiously attempting to build a complete collection of commercially available phonodiscs dealing with black history. The list is intended primarily as a local-use reference tool, but it is also useful as a purchase guide on a wider basis.

40. **A Bookless Curriculum,** by Roland G. Brown. Cebco Standard Publishing, Cebco Pflaum, 9 Kulick Rd., Fairfield, NJ 07006. 1972. $5.65. 134p.

*Scope:* A report on an experimental program for teaching English to tenth and twelfth grade students "who are the potential dropouts, the failures, the nonreaders, the school haters" (Objectives, p. 11). Units of the course were built around 47 motion pictures used thematically plus brief attempts at filmmaking, TV production, and sound production. The objectives of the experiment, the instruments used, the teaching methods followed, the conclusions, and the films are all fully described.

*Arrangement:* By theme.

*Entries:* Unit number, theme, film title, teaching method and questions about the film, synopsis and critical comments, approximate time of unit.

*Special Features:* Questionnaire for English students; student opinionaires; statistical analyses; student evaluations of films viewed; curriculum cost sheet; bibliography; film list and sources.

41. **Career Development Resource Materials K-6,** prepared by the Project team of the Independent School District No.623 Roseville Area Schools. Published by the Pupil Personnel Service Section, Minnesota Department of Education, St. Paul, MN. Available from Documents Section, Room 140 Centennial Building, St. Paul, MN 55155. 1972. $1. Payment must accompany order. 52p. Available also in microfiche and hard copy from ERIC Document Reproduction Service, P.O. Box 190, Arlington, VA 22210. Apply for current prices. ED 117 292.

*Scope:* Approximately 400 titles of books, films, filmstrips, kits, records, and specimen sets are included in this selected list. All of the materials were reviewed by members of the Project team; only those titles that are fairly direct in their approach were judged worthy of inclusion. Review sources for each title are indicated when available. Materials are divided into three categories—personal development, the world of work, and occupations. Each category is subdivided by specific subject headings or by specific occupations; grade levels and descriptive annotations are included.

*Arrangement:* By subject, then by Dewey Decimal Classification number.

*Entries:* Classification number, author (books), title, publisher/producer/distributor, date (books), length in minutes/number of items, rental/purchase price, annotation, grade level, review source.

42. **Career Development Resources: A Bibliography of Audio-Visual and Printed Materials K-12,** compiled by the Lake Superior Regional Resource Center Staff, Kenneth Held, Director. Personnel Services Section, Division of Instruction, Minnesota Department of Education, St. Paul, MN. Available from Documents Section, Room 140, Centennial Building, St. Paul, MN 55155. 1975. $5. Payment must accompany order. 104p. Available also in microfiche and hard copy from ERIC Document Reproduction Service, P.O. Box 190, Arlington, VA 22210. Apply for current prices. ED 117 292.

*Scope:* A list of recent career education resource materials for students and teachers—including books, tapes, cassettes with books and other printed materials, filmstrips, slides, kits, games, posters, pictures, and subscriptions. Grade levels range from kindergarten through college and adult. The materials are briefly described but not evaluated; they are on display and may be evaluated at the Career Education Resource Center, Lake Superior Area, Duluth, Minnesota.

*Arrangement:* Alphabetical by abbreviation of manufacturer, then alphabetical by title.

*Entries:* Manufacturer's abbreviation, reference number, catalog number if provided by manufacturer, distributor, title, cost, copyright or production date, type of medium, description of content, grade level range.

*Special Features:* Four indexes, each on different colored paper: abbreviation, title, type of medium, grade level.

43. **Career Development Resources: A Guide to Audiovisual and Printed Materials for Grades K-12,** by Harry N. Drier, Jr. Charles A. Jones Publications, Wadsworth Publishing Co., Belmont, CA 94002. 1973. $11.95. 301p. (An expansion of *K-12 Guide for Integrating Career De-*

*velopment Into Local Curriculum* developed for the Wisconsin Department of Public Instruction, 1972)

*Scope:* The materials in this guide were selected by counselors and teachers in grades K-12 to meet learning objectives in three areas of career education: self-understanding, the world of work, and career planning and preparation. Planned as a reference tool for classroom teachers, librarians, and media personnel, the work includes approximately 2,200 titles of films, filmstrips, records, slides, tapes, kits, games, books, and other printed materials which have been used by teachers from across the country.

*Arrangement:* By grade levels, then by subject areas of career education, then by type of medium followed by individual titles and series titles.

*Entries:* Title or series title, author, publisher/producer/distributor, date if available, color or b/w, rental/purchase price, brief descriptive annotation.

*Special Features:* Resource categories index; publishers and producers directory; career development bibliography. Book design allows space for adding locally produced and new commercial products.

44. **Career Education Instructional Materials Guide for Teachers: Kindergarten Through Grade Twelve,** by Richard O. Peters. New Hampshire Supervisory School Union 58, Experimental School Project, Groveton, NH 03104. Available in microfiche and hard copy from ERIC Reproduction Service, P.O. Box 190, Arlington, VA 22210. 1975. Apply for current prices. 22p. ED 110 723.

*Scope:* A selected list of filmstrips, films, cassettes, posters, multimedia kits, textbooks, manuals, transparencies, and workbooks selected for the purpose of providing students with a wide variety of sensory as well as affective, cognitive, and psychomotor domain information and experiences. Entries are briefly described but not evaluated.

*Arrangement:* By grade levels.

*Entries:* Series title, grade level, type of medium, number of units, purpose, individual titles in the series, source.

*Special Features:* List of sources from which materials may be obtained; "Other Ideas."

45. **Career Education Resource Guide: Michigan.** Michigan State Department of Education, Lansing, MI 48901, in cooperation with the Royal Oak, Michigan, City School District. Available in microfiche and hard copy from ERIC Document Reproduction Service, P.O. Box

190, Arlington, VA 22210. 1975. Apply for current prices. 407p. ED 118 951.

*Scope:* A team of teachers, counselors, and support personnel through-out Michigan evaluated the materials in this bibliography and in many cases tested their usefulness in classrooms. The types of media included are books and other printed materials, charts, films, filmstrips, filmloops, games and simulations, records, slides, transparencies, and teacher guides. The first section of the bibliography is on professional development and the materials are grouped into four career development components: self-awareness and assessment, career awareness and exploration, career decision making and planning, and career planning and placement. Each component group is preceded by a Quick Content Reference Index and is then further divided into grade levels from K-10. The second section, professional readings (12 pages), lists references on career education under the following headings: bibliographies, directories, and indexes; books; information services; current journal articles; monographs; pamphlets and papers.

*Arrangement:* By topics and grade levels as indicated above. The grade level groups in the first section are further divided by types of media followed by titles in alphabetical order.

*Entries:* First section—title or series title, author (print), publisher, date, distributor, type of medium, length, price if known, career development component in code grade level, reading level, suggested curriculum use in code, annotation.

*Special Features:* List of producers of educational materials; evaluation sheet.

46. **Cassette Books.** 2d ed. Reference and Information, Division for the Blind and Physically Handicapped, Library of Congress, Washington, DC 20542. 1974. Free. 146p.

*Scope:* This catalog supersedes all earlier cassette book catalogs and lists approximately 1,200 annotated titles—all cassette books issued since 1968 and available on free loan from libraries which offer services to the blind. Subjects include: philosophy, psychology, religion, social sciences, English language, science, technology, medical science, physical fitness, domestic arts, the arts, recreation, literature, history, geography, biography and travel. Included also are: fiction, books in foreign languages—French, German, Spanish, and Yiddish—and children's books.

*Arrangement:* Alphabetical by title under Dewey Decimal Classification numbers and headings with additional sections for fiction, foreign language books, and children's books—also alphabetical by title.

*Entries:* Title, author, reader, number of cassettes, producer, cassette book number, descriptive annotation, grade level (for children's books).

*Special Features:* Directions and forms for ordering cassette books; helpful hints for cassette handling; author/title index.

47. **Catalog of Audio-Visual Aids in Hypertension.** High Blood Pressure Information Center, 120/80 National Institutes of Health, Bethesda, MD 20014. Available from the Superintendent of Documents, U.S. Government Printing Office, Washington, DC 20402. 1975. $2.90. 110p. (DHEW Publication no.75–719)

*Scope:* An annotated list of 50 films, 23 videotape cassettes, and 18 slide sets, audiotapes, and cassettes produced by government and nongovernment agencies and private companies. Every entry has been checked for its availability and description and should be available from the address included. However, a listing "does not constitute an endorsement by the National High Blood Pressure Education Program of its accuracy of content, clarity or visual appeal" (Introduction). Includes materials for the general public, for patient education, and for professional use.

*Arrangement:* Six broad subject headings are subdivided by type of medium, followed by titles arranged alphabetically (for the most part) with each entry on a separate page.

*Entries:* Title, author, brief description of content, length, type of medium, color or b/w, sound, recommended audience, order number, name and address of source, free loan or rental price, purchase price, preview conditions, additional materials if any, and price.

48. **Catalog of Educational Captioned Films for the Deaf,** prepared by the Special Office for Materials Distribution, Division of Media Services, Bureau of Education for the Handicapped, Office of Education, U.S. Department of Health, Education and Welfare, Washington, DC 20202. 1976. Apply. 116p.

*Scope:* The purposes of the Captioned Films for the Deaf Program, as set forth in the federal law, are threefold: "(1) to bring to deaf persons understanding and appreciation of those films which play an important part in the general and cultural advancement of hearing persons; (2) to provide, through these films, enriched educational and cultural experiences through which deaf persons can be brought into better touch with the realities of their environment; and (3) to provide a wholesome and rewarding experience which deaf persons may share together" (Purposes of the Captioned Films Program—P.L.85–905). This catalog lists and describes approximately 800 16mm films on a wide variety of subjects, available for use with the deaf, and suitable for primary, intermediate, and advanced interest or age levels.

*Arrangement:* Alphabetical by title.

*Entries:* Title, educational captioned film number, running time, color or b/w, whether or not sound track is synchronized with captions or a nonverbal film, descriptive annotation, series title, subject headings, interest level(s), producer and distributor in code, date, lesson guide where additional information may be obtained, and page number in guide.

*Special Features:* Obligations of borrowers; care of films; alphabetical list of subject headings and see references; captioned films reserve collection; key to abbreviations used for producers and distributors.

49. **A Catalog of Nonprint Materials Useful in Computer Related Instruction,** compiled and edited by Ben Jones, Oregon Total Information System, Lane County Intermediate Education District, Eugene, OR. Available in microfiche and hard copy from ERIC Document Reproduction Service, P.O. Box 190, Arlington, VA 22210. 1973. Apply for current prices. 66p. ED 096 976.

*Scope:* A list of 175 titles of films, filmstrips, audiotapes, and records in the field of computer science education. The author drew upon the following sources in compiling the list: collections in school instructional media centers, catalogs of data processing associations, and vendors' catalogs; he aimed to make the list as comprehensive as possible and to provide subject access to the materials. Evaluations are not included.

*Arrangement:* Alphabetical by title.

*Entries:* Title, grade level, type of medium, length, color or b/w, series title if any, description of content, distributor, rental cost.

*Special Features:* Subject index; sources for materials.

50. **Chicorel Index to Poetry in Collections on Discs, Tapes and Cassettes,** edited by Marietta Chicorel. Chicorel Library Publishing Corp., 275 Central Park West, New York, NY 10024. 1972. $60. 443p. (Chicorel Index Series v.4)

*Scope:* Approximately 700 collections of poetry recorded in English on more than 1,800 discs, audiotapes, and cassettes are indexed in this volume. Over 25,000 entries provide access to the recordings by title, first line, poet, reader/actor, and director. A companion volume is an index to poetry in anthologies in print, volume 5 A/B/C, listing all available and recent materials. No volume in this series supersedes any other; there is no duplication in content as each volume contains entirely new material. Volume 4 indexes recordings of poetry written by and for children, epic poetry, current social protest, satires and limericks, international poetry in translation, poems included in literature collections and in textbooks, full poetry texts and abridgments, poems ranging in period from antiquity to the present.

*Arrangement:* One alphabetical sequence including all types of entries with main entry under album title.

*Entries:* Album title, author, director, performer, translator, subject indicators, price, year of release, number of discs/reels/cassettes/ cartridges/filmloops, sound reproduction requirements, record label, order number, contents titles with authors, Library of Congress catalog card number if any.

*Special Features:* Subject indicator section with title references; author list; album title list; poems listed by title/first line; performers list; director/editor list; Shakespeare's Sonnets; producer/distributor addresses; glossary of technical terms.

51. **Chicorel Index to the Spoken Arts on Discs, Tapes and Cassettes,** edited by Marietta Chicorel. Chicorel Library Publishing Corp., 275 Central Park West, New York, NY 10024. 1973, 1974. $60 per volume. 3v. (Chicorel Index Series, v.7, v.7A, v.7B)

*Scope:* These companion volumes provide indexes to plays, short stories, essays, novels, speeches, commentaries, conversations, poetry, and readings recorded on discs, tapes, and cassettes. The first volume analyzes more than 1,000 collections with approximately 6,000 entries and a strong emphasis on plays. The second volume also has approximately 6,000 entries and emphasizes poetry. The third volume enlarges the coverage of the first two and contains about 9,000 entries. The dictionary catalog arrangement provides multiple access points—album title, title of work, author, performer/dramatic company/reader/speaker, editor, director. The indexed materials range in level from elementary and high school through college and university. No volume in the series supersedes any other; each contains all new materials.

*Arrangement:* One alphabetical sequence including all types of entries with main entry under album title.

*Entries:* Album title, editor/director, performer/dramatic company/ reader/speaker, contents titles with authors, translator, subject indicators, annotation, price, number of discs/tapes, sound reproduction requirements, record label, producer/distributor, manufacturer's order number, Library of Congress catalog card number if any.

*Special Features:* Ten back-of-book indexes which list: album title, author; poems, by title or first line; spoken arts, including short stories, novels, speeches, commentaries, essays, conversations, and readings; editor/director; performer/dramatic company/reader/speaker; a subject guide; producers/distributors, with addresses; glossary of technical terms; a list of subject indicators to album title references.

52. **China: A Resource and Curriculum Guide,** edited by Arlene Posner and Arne J. deKeijzer. 2d ed. University of Chicago Press, 5801 Ellis Ave., Chicago, IL 60637. 1976. $3.95 paper; $15 cloth. 317p.

*Scope:* This revised and expanded edition is divided into three parts. The first section includes three essays on teaching about China: Edward Friedman's "Teaching Materials on Contemporary China: A Critical Evaluation"; Jonathan Spence's "Adapting Scholarly Work to the Needs of Educators"; and David L. Weitzman's "Teaching about China in the Classroom: What We Look for Beyond Seeing." Part 2, Materials on China, contains curriculum units as well as audiovisual and printed materials currently available and "offering representative views of the social, economic, political, and cultural aspects of China's society and international relations, both past and present." A new section, part 3, lists materials from the People's Republic of China "because it is important to evaluate another culture on its own terms . . ." (Preface). In the two latter sections, the audiovisual materials included are mostly films and filmstrips; the printed resources include books, packets of materials, periodicals and scholarly journals, newsletters, monographs, and papers.
*Arrangement:* Parts 2 and 3 are arranged by type of medium, then alphabetically by title.
*Entries:* Title or series title, length in minutes/frames/pages, color or b/w, sound or silent, author/publisher/producer/distributor, prices, subject, audience level, description of content and evaluation.
*Special Features:* Advisory Board for this Volume; Introduction by Edwin O. Reischauer, stressing the need for this type of study; list of audiovisual distributors; list of publishers; index.

53. **CINE Golden Eagle Film Awards.** Council on International Nontheatrical Events, 1201 Sixteenth St., N.W., Washington, DC 20036. Annual. 1953 to date. $3.50 postpaid.

*Scope:* Approximately 200–250 CINE Golden Eagle films selected by CINE evaluating procedures, in accordance with regulations specified in the yearbook, from among more than 750 entries from the United States as outstanding examples of film productions in such areas as: agriculture, animation, amateur adult, amateur youth, architecture, the arts, business and industry, education, experimental/avant-garde, history-anthropology-archeology, maritime, medical, public health, safety, science and technology, social documentary and religion, sports, theatrical short subjects, travel and tourism—exploration, and television and short documentary. Evaluative criteria recommended by CINE for use by evaluators in rating films include: imagination, creativeness, and cinematographic excellence; authenticity, honesty, and sensitivity; presentation of the United States, other countries, their people and institutions, in a fair and objective manner; brevity in telling point; experimental and unique approaches; ability to be understood by a variety of international audiences or by specialized international audiences; new insights into the subject, imparting a sense of revelation; and visual imagery, with image and sound in artistic unity.

*Arrangement:* Alphabetical by title.

*Entries:* Title, length; color or b/w; sponsor; producer; production credits including names of such staff as director, editor, cameraman, composer, narrator, sound technician, art and animation technicians, etc.; 20-60 word descriptions of content; Library of Congress catalog card number.

*Special Features:* Introduction by CINE President; explanation of CINE's role, sponsors and awards system and ceremonies; CINE patrons; CINE international honors; CINE Eagle films produced by adult amateurs; international calendar of festivals in which American films were entered through CINE; instructions and requirements for submitting films to CINE; CINE jurors; list of producers, sponsors, and distributors; index of credits; CINE 1975–76 officers and directors.

54. **Cities,** by Dwight W. Hoover. R. R. Bowker Co., 1180 Avenue of the Americas, New York, NY 10036. 1976. $14.95 plus shipping and handling. 231p. (Bibliographic Guides for Contemporary Collections)

*Scope:* A list of over 1,000 critically annotated books, journals, games, films, filmstrips, audiotapes, cassettes, kits, slides, and transparencies on all aspects of the American urban experience. The main criteria for inclusion were contemporaneity and availability of materials. Out-of-print books and films or filmstrips more than 10 years old were omitted, with a few exceptions because of quality. The materials range from elementary, junior high school, and high school to adult, specialist, and advanced reader audience levels. The bibliography is divided into two parts. The first is concerned with materials about present-day dilemmas of cities—general problems, blacks, ethnic groups, housing, education, transportation, urbanization and suburbanization, crime and the police, civil disorders, urban poverty, urban bosses, reform, and the provision of services. The second part includes materials concerned with the various disciplines which have studied the city—urban theory, images, architecture, planning, sociology, geography, history, economics, government, and urban biographies. The author introduces each subject area with brief comments about the background of the problem and the nature of the materials listed.

*Arrangement:* By subjects mentioned above, then alphabetical by author or title.

*Entries:* Author, title or series title, publisher/producer/distributor, date, type of medium (nonprint), color or b/w, length in pages/ minutes/items, sound or captioned, individual titles if a series, rental and purchase prices, Library of Congress card catalog number if available, descriptive-evaluative annotation including suggested audiences and uses, narrator/translator/other credits when appropriate.

*Special Features:* Selected list of journals on urban themes; producer/ distributor directory; author index; title index.

55. **Classical Music Recordings for Home and Library,** by Richard S. Halsey. American Library Association, 50 E. Huron St., Chicago, IL 60611. 1976. $15. 340p.

*Scope:* More than 4,000 sound recordings, selected from over 43,000 recorded compositions issued in the United States during the period 1961–75 are evaluated in this discography and selection tool. Categories of music represented are: arias, art songs, chamber and orchestral pieces, choral, electronic, experimental, keyboard works, Gregorian chants, operas, and symphonies. Titles are coded to indicate listening levels (elementary, secondary, advanced), aesthetic significance, and relative popularity. Also cited are notable, generally recommended, or best available recorded versions for each title, as well as the accessibility rating for composers' works. "Documentation and verification of ratings, running times, critical opinion, and textual information took five years to complete and involved scholarly, technical, institutional, and commercial resources in the United States, Canada, and England. Ratings for titles and specific recorded versions were reached by . . . consensus judgments of musicologists and eminent reviewers" (*ALA Publications 1976*, p. 16). In addition to the discography, the book covers all aspects of the development and administration of a record collection: order preparation; vendor selection; the characteristics of sound recording literature, including books, major review journals and indexes; acquisition and budgeting procedures; a comparative analysis of cataloging and classification systems; care of recordings, equipment and environments for listening.

*Arrangement:* Composer-title list is arranged by type-of-music categories, then by guide numbers and composers in alphabetical order. Manufacturer's catalog number-performer list is alphabetical by manufacturer.

*Entries:* Guide number, composer, title, age minima, aesthetic significance code, access code number, length in minutes, label and label number.

*Special Features:* Glossary of audio terms; title index to composer-title list; subject, proper name, and composer index.

56. **Compendium of Noncommercially Prepared Nonprint Resources in Educational Personnel Preparation,** by Wesley C. Meierhenry. ERIC Clearinghouse on Teacher Education, Washington, DC 20036. Available in microfiche and hard copy from ERIC Document Reproduction Service, P.O. Box 190, Arlington, VA 22210. 1974. Apply for current prices. 267p. ED 092 485.

*Scope:* A comprehensive catalog of nonprint materials produced by institutional or nonprofit agencies and concerned with preservice and inservice preparation of educational personnel. Included are audio cassettes, tape reels and phonodiscs; games and simulation; motion pictures; multimedia; slides, filmstrips, tapes; and videotapes. The information about these products was gathered from all segments of the educational community on a standard form designed and used originally in the author's 1970 publication *Mediated Teacher Education Resources.* Some of the subjects included are: behavior, classroom environment, curriculum development, disadvantaged youth, early childhood education, educational innovation, educational technology, elementary education, exceptional children, language arts, nongraded system, open education, protocol materials, reading, student teacher relationship, teacher behavior, teacher education, teaching methods, and urban environment. The descriptive annotations are those furnished by producers of the materials.

*Arrangement:* By type of medium, then alphabetical by title.

*Entries:* Title, type of medium, producer, distributor, date, length in minutes, cost, whether suitable for preservice or inservice use, related material if any, brief description of content.

*Special Features:* Appendix A, Survey Form; Appendix B, Title List by Medium; Appendix C, Distributors; Subject Index; About ERIC.

**57. A Core Media Collection for Secondary Schools,** by Lucy G. Brown. R. R. Bowker Co., 1180 Avenue of the Americas, New York, NY 10036. 1975. $16.95. 221p.

*Scope:* A selected list of approximately 2,000 titles of audiotapes, films, filmstrips, filmloops, kits, phonodiscs, prints, specimens, and models recommended for use in grades 7–12. The author evaluated the materials on the basis of their authenticity, technical quality, appropriateness for the subjects being considered, student level, interest and motivation, accuracy in content, and validity in treatment. Many items included have received favorable reviews in professional journals and are so designated. Most selections were produced between 1965 and February 1974. Titles highly recommended for early acquisition when building a media collection are preceded by an asterisk.

*Arrangement:* Alphabetical by subject with frequent cross references, using *Sears List of Subject Headings,* then alphabetical by title.

*Entries:* Title, type of medium, format description, producer/distributor, date of release, title of series, contents note, recommending sources, price (1974), order number, grade levels, Dewey Decimal Classification number.

*Special Features:* Title index; directory of producers and distributors; recommending sources.

*Author's Note:* A revised edition of a companion volume, *Resources for Learning: A Core Media Collection for Elementary Schools,* edited by Roderick McDaniel (R. R. Bowker Co., 1971), is planned for 1978.

**58. Critical Index of Films on Man and His Environment,** by the Conservation Education Association. Available from the Interstate Printers & Publishers, Inc., 19–27 N. Jackson St., Danville, IL 61832. 1972. $1.25 less educational discount. 32p. *Supplement.* 1972. Supplied free with basic volume. (Supersedes *Critical Index of Films and Filmstrips in Conservation*). (Education . . . Key to Conservation Series no. 8)

*Scope:* A selected list of films which are considered to be the "best visual aids to assist teachers and others interested in imparting a better understanding on the interrelationships of man and his environment" (cover). Some of the recommendations in the original *Critical Index* appear again in this publication because they are considered to be of good quality and still valid. The new selections were made by 20 members of the Conservation Education Association and other experts in the use of audiovisual materials; they were assisted in evaluating the films by panels from 13 institutions.

Audience levels range from kindergarten through college and adult groups. Titles are grouped according to categories: the natural environment, man's impact on the environment, and some solutions.

*Arrangement:* By three broad categories mentioned above, then by subheadings, then alphabetical by title.

*Entries:* Title, series title if any, running time, audience level, description of content, evaluation, distributor, date.

*Special Features:* TV programs produced by NBC, CBS, and ABC networks; list of distributors; tabular index by audience level, title, and subject.

59. **Cultures in the North: Aleut, Athabascan Indian, Eskimo, Haida Indian, Tlingit Indian, Tsimpshian Indian: Multi-Media Resource List,** compiled by Sarah A. Isto. Alaska Educational Program for Intercultural Communication, Center for Northern Educational Research, University of Alaska, Fairbanks, AK 99701. 1975. Apply. 46p. Available also in microfiche and hard copy from ERIC Document Reproduction Service, P.O. Box 190, Arlington, VA 22210. Apply for current prices. ED 108 809.

*Scope:* A wide variety of titles of books, periodicals, films, filmstrips, slides, and miscellaneous media are included in this annotated list which is intended to assist teachers in identifying, collecting, and assessing useful materials on the Alaskan native cultures. All books included were examined and evaluated according to criteria of relevance, accuracy, interest to students, quality of writing, attitude toward the culture being described, freedom from stereotyping and condescension, and suitability for use by students in grades 1 through 12. Approximately 1,200 books were examined and about 400 selected for inclusion. The audiovisual materials were selected from catalogs and were not previewed or evaluated; therefore, teachers are cautioned to examine them critically.

*Arrangement:* By cultural group, then by type of medium; books are listed alphabetically by author; periodicals and nonprint, alphabetically by title.

*Entries:* Author (books), title, series title, publisher/producer/distributor, date (books only), length in pages/minutes/frames/slides, color or b/w, descriptive annotation, grade level.

*Special Features:* Resources for teachers; title index; line drawing illustrations.

60. **Data Processing Film Catalogue,** by Lois A. White. Memphis State University, Memphis, TN 38117. Available from Society for Data Educators, 983 Fairmeadow Rd., Memphis, TN 38117. 1975. $1.95. 20p.

*Scope:* A list of 205 motion pictures selected to aid teachers of data processing at all levels in learning and teaching about automation.

*Arrangement:* Alphabetical by title.

*Entries:* Title, level(s), source, date, running time, sound or silent, color or b/w, availability information, descriptive annotation, keyword numbers used to describe subject matter of film.

*Special Features:* Addresses for ordering films.

61. **David Sohn's Film Notes on Selected Short Films,** by David A. Sohn. Cebco Standard Publishing, Cebco Pflaum, 9 Kulick Rd., Fairfield, NJ 07006. 1975. $3.75. 113p.

*Scope:* Critical reviews of more than 100 short films which the author describes as "part of the cream of the filmmaking crop" (Introduction). All of the selections have been found valuable by the author in teaching students to observe, to write better, and to discuss matters of importance. Throughout the text, practical comments about the short film and its uses are interwoven with film theory. Suggested audience levels range from kindergarten through high school and college. The topical or curriculum areas in which the films can be useful include language arts, humanities, social studies, science, mathematics, film study, and psychology.

*Arrangement:* Alphabetical by title.

*Entries:* Title, running time, color or b/w, suggested topical or curriculum areas, distributor, audience levels.

*Special Features:* Index to films by distributor; directory of distributors; subject, author, and filmmaker index; illustrations from the films.

62. **The Development of a Bibliography of Library Skills Instructional Resources,** by Margret A. Iadanza. Department of Library Science, Central Michigan University, 105 Park Library, Mt. Pleasant, MI 48859. Available in microfiche and hard copy from ERIC Document Reproduction Service, P.O. Box 190, Arlington, VA 22210. 1975. Apply for current prices. 72p. ED 114 085.

*Scope:* A comprehensive list of more than 1,000 titles of films, filmstrips, audio materials, programmed instruction media, slides, graphics, masters, transparencies, multimedia kits, and supplementary printed aids (excluding textbooks) which were culled from the catalogs of approximately 368 producers and distributors as of May 1, 1975. These data were entered into a computer for ease in updating and for retrieval by title, by type of medium, and by the following subjects: general, cataloging and classification, library courtesy, history of books and libraries, use of nonprint media, and use of reference materials. The entries consist of one line of computer print and are not annotated.

*Arrangement:* In three sections—alphabetical by title, by type of medium, and by subject area.

*Entries:* Title, series title, number of titles in series, subject in code, audience, type of medium.

*Special Features:* Bibliography of related literature; form for requesting catalogs; key to source code; alphabetical list of sources.

63. **Developmental Guidance Materials for the Elementary School,** by Gene Sauter, edited by G. Dean Miller. Rev. ed. Pupil Personnel Services Section, Minnesota Department of Education, St. Paul, MN. Available from Documents Section, Room 140, Centennial Building, St. Paul, MN 55155. 1974. $2. Payment must accompany order. 101p.

*Scope:* An awareness list of books and other printed materials, filmstrips, cassettes, multimedia kits, games, and simulations designed for guidance and vocational programs at the elementary school level. The list is divided into two categories—general developmental guidance materials and vocational awareness materials. With a few exceptions, inservice materials for teachers and personal growth activities for parents are not included; nor does the author consider the bibliography to be either "a complete or a current listing of *all* of the materials that can be utilized in a guidance program" (Introduction). Criteria for inclusion are not stated, nor are the materials evaluated. Some of the materials have been field tested by their producers, but for only three of the programs included was it possible to locate specific research results.

*Arrangement:* By two broad categories, then by title or program/series title.

*Entries:* Title, author, rationale/objectives, publisher/producer, date, type of medium/program, suggested grade level, suggested retail price, materials/components, topics covered, method of teaching, presentation time, research if available.

*Special Features:* Table of Contents is a tabular index providing access to materials by title, grade levels, and types of media.

64. **Directory of Audiovisual Training Materials,** compiled by Thomas Wilds. The Council for Exceptional Children, 1920 Association Dr., Reston, VA 22091. 1974. $4.25. 120p. (Handicapped Children in Head Start Series). Available also in hard copy and microfiche from ERIC Document Reproduction Service, P.O. Box 190, Arlington, VA 22210. Apply for current prices. ED 091 881.

*Scope:* A selected list of 265 16mm films, filmstrips, slides, cassettes, and videotapes for use in training Head Start staff concerning the special needs of young handicapped children. The titles were selected from the catalogs of university film distribution centers and from other lists.

*Arrangement:* Alphabetical by title.

*Entries:* Title or series title, length, color or b/w, type of medium, date if available, descriptive annotation, individual titles if a series, producer, distributor, free loan/rental and sale prices, Library of Congress catalog card number if available.

*Special Features:* Index to subject headings; subject guide; guide to producers and distributors; material referral sheet.

65. **Directory of Spoken-Voice Audio-Cassettes,** edited and published by Gerald McKee. Cassette Information Services, Box 17727, Los Angeles, CA 90057. 1976. $10 prepaid; $11 if billed. 168p. Revised annually and updated in the quarterly CIS *Audio-Cassette Newsletter.* $6 per year prepaid; $7 per year if billed.

*Scope:* These spoken-voice recorded programs are concerned with a wide variety of subjects and are designed for the adult or college-level listener. However, the names and addresses of companies that produce educational and entertainment cassettes for children are listed in a new section in this edition. Excluded from the *Directory* are cassettes in the humor category and those programs which incorporate slides and filmstrips, since it is the editor's purpose to emphasize the cassette as a convenient educational medium without the need for visual equipment. The entries are briefly described; almost all are available by mail order.

*Arrangement:* Alphabetical by names of producers.

*Entries:* Title or series title, length, description of content, number of cassettes in series, order number when available, price.

*Special Features:* Title and subject index.

66. **Discovering Music: Where To Start on Records and Tapes—the Great Composers and their Works—Today's Major Recording Artists,** by Roy Hemming. Four Winds Press, Scholastic Magazines, Inc., 50 W. Forty-fourth St., New York, NY 10036. 1974. $14.95. 379p.

*Scope:* As the title suggests, this work is made up of three parts. In the first section the author interviews fifty leading musicians—conductors, soloists, composers, teachers—and each recommends pieces of music he or she considers best for starting a record collection. The second section is concerned with fifty composers and their major works, from baroque to avant-garde. For each composer there is a brief biography followed by descriptions of his or her works and critical evaluations of the best available recordings of these works on stereophonic and quadrasonic records, cassettes, and cartridges. In the final section, established recording artists and promising newcomers are discussed, followed by lists of their best recordings. In this section also the author surveys the major American and European orchestras which record regularly. The book is written in nontechnical language as a guide for those who want to get started building their own record collections.

*Arrangement:* In three parts mentioned above, then alphabetical by name of composer or performing artist.

*Entries:* Composer, title, performing artist or group, conductor, label and number, whether disc or cassette, whether mono/stereo/quadrasonic, critical comments.

*Special Features:* Photos of composers and artists; pronunciations of surnames; information about recording systems currently available; glossary of musical terms; index.

67. **Discovery in Film Book Two: A Teacher Sourcebook,** by Malcolm W. Gordon. Paulist Press, 545 Island Rd., Ramsey, NJ 07446. 1973. $5.95. 162p.

*Scope:* The aim of this book is "for both quality and variety in the films it treats" (Introduction). It is as "comprehensive as possible in including the major areas and styles of 16mm films," e.g., documentaries, animated, photojournalistic, experimental, avant-garde, social, and anthropological films. For every film included, at least two were rejected by the author.

*Arrangement:* By broad subject headings (communication, freedom, peace, love, happiness), then randomly by title.

*Entries:* Title, summary of content, critical review, running time, color or b/w, rental/purchase prices, distributor number, suggestions for use, questions, and resource readings.

*Special Features:* Photographic illustrations from the films; addresses of film distribution centers; index of films; Appendix 1, Some Suggestions for a Super-8 Film Making Course; Appendix 2, List of Film Distributors.

68. **Drug Abuse Films,** by Joan Grupenhoff. 3d ed. National Coordinating Council on Drug Education, 1211 Connecticut Ave., N.W., Suite 212, Washington, DC 20036. Distributed by the American Library Association, 50 E. Huron St., Chicago, IL 60611. 1973. $5. 119p.

*Scope:* There are 192 titles of films, filmstrips, records, cassettes, and transparency sets in this evaluative report by the NCCDE which systematically reviews drug abuse audiovisual materials for scientific accuracy and conceptual integrity. The report reflects "the confusion, hysteria, and misconceptions that characterize the majority of existing drug abuse education programs" (Preface). Thirty-one percent of the titles are classified "unacceptable" because they are "inaccurate, distorted, outdated, and conceptually unsound." Fifty-three percent are placed in a "restricted" category; only 16 percent are judged to be scientifically and conceptually acceptable. A separate section of the report lists a small number of filmstrips, films, cassettes, and transparencies developed for minority groups; a special panel found these titles to be of poor quality—all reinforcing existing stereotypes and invalid generalizations about drug use among racial minorities.

*Arrangement:* By categories mentioned above, then alphabetical by title.

*Entries:* Title, type of medium, date, audience (except for "unacceptable" titles), producer, distributor, rental/purchase price, length, color or b/w, sound, accompanying guide if any, date of review, synopsis, evaluation.

*Special Features:* NCCDE review process; how to select a drug abuse film; evaluation panel members; background on NCCDE; member organizations; alphabetical index to films and audiovisuals.

69. **Drug and Health Mediagraphy: Personal Health,** by Ralph R. Dykstra, in conjunction with Peter J. Dirr. Research and Development Complex, Faculty of Professional Studies, State University College at Buffalo, 1300 Elmwood Ave., Buffalo, NY 14222. 1974. Apply. 87p. Available also in microfiche only from ERIC Document Reproduction Service, P.O. Box 190, Arlington, VA 22210. Apply for current price. ED 106 992.

*Scope:* The first in a series of selected bibliographies on health, this list includes approximately 400 films, filmstrips, articles, books, kits, models, pamphlets, pictures, records, slides, and miscellaneous media. All entries were "suggested by teachers after careful screening, including evaluation with handicapped children" (Introduction). Materials are grouped around four main headings concerned primarily with personal health: dental health, first aid and survival, nutrition, safety education.

*Arrangement:* By four main subject headings listed above, then by type of medium, followed by titles in alphabetical order.

*Entries:* Title or series title, recommended chronological age range, recommended mental age range, date, length in minutes/frames/slides/pages, color or b/w, free loan/cost, author (printed materials), periodical with date and pages (articles), distributor/pub-lisher/producer, abstract.

*Special Features:* Names and addresses of distributors.

70. **Drug and Health Mediagraphy II: Mental Health,** by Ralph R. Dykstra, in conjunction with Peter J. Dirr. Research and Development Complex, Faculty of Professional Studies, State University College at Buffalo, 1300 Elmwood Ave., Buffalo, NY 14222. 1974. Apply. 127p. Available also in microfiche only from ERIC Document Reproduction Service, P.O. Box 190, Arlington, VA 22210. Apply for current price. ED 106 993.

*Scope:* The second in a series of selected bibliographies on health, this list includes approximately 350 articles, books, book/record combinations, films, filmstrips, periodicals, photographs, records, study prints, and transparencies. All materials in the list were "sug-gested by teachers after careful screening, including evaluation with handicapped children" (Introduction), and span a variety of topics and ability levels.

*Arrangement:* By type of medium in the above-mentioned order, then alphabetical by title.

*Entries:* Title or series title, recommended chronological age range, recommended mental age range, date, length in minutes/frames/slides/pages, color or b/w, free loan/cost, author (printed mate-rials), periodical with date and pages (articles), distributor/pub-lisher/producer, abstract.

*Special Features:* Names and addresses of distributors.

71. **Educators Guide to Free Films,** compiled and edited by Mary Foley Horkheimer and John C. Diffor with W. D. Phillipson. 36th ed. Edu-cators Progress Service, Randolph, WI 53956. 1976. $12.75. 716p. Re-vised annually. (For use during the school year 1976–77)

*Scope:* Motion pictures in all instructional subjects, including accident prevention, agriculture, aerospace education, business education, geography, health, history, home economics, music, and science. Currently available free of charge on loan to school superintendents, teachers, audiovisual instructors, and librarians are 4,246 titles.

*Arrangement:* By subject categories, then alphabetical by title.

*Entries:* Title, distributor, date, running time, silent or sound, color or b/w, availability, descriptive annotation in 10–70 words.

*Special Features:* Source and availability index gives terms of loan and length of time necessary for booking; title index; detailed sub-ject index; television clearance; Australian availability index; Ca-nadian availability index; various sections of the *Guide* distin-guished by different colored paper.

72. **Educators Guide to Free Filmstrips,** compiled and edited by Mary Foley Horkheimer and John C. Diffor. 28th ed. Educators Progress Service, Randolph, WI 53956. 1976. $10. 168p. Revised annually. (For use during the school year 1976–77)

*Scope:* Filmstrips, slides, and transparencies in all instructional subjects currently available free of charge, either on loan or as gifts. There are 481 titles including 266 filmstrips, 214 sets of slides, and 1 set of transparencies.

*Arrangement:* By subject categories, then alphabetical by title.

*Entries:* Title, distributor, date, length in number of frames/slides, availability of script or sound accompaniment, silent or sound, color or b/w, descriptive annotation.

*Special Features:* Introduction gives suggestions on how to use filmstrips and how to obtain them; title index; detailed subject index; source and availability index gives terms of loan and length of time necessary for booking for each distributor; Australian availability index; Canadian availability index; various sections of the *Guide* distinguished by use of different colored paper.

73. **Educators Guide to Free Guidance Materials,** compiled and edited by Mary H. Saterstrom with Gail F. Farwell. 15th ed. Educators Progress Service, Randolph, WI 53956. 1976. $10.75. 395p. Revised annually. (For use during the school year 1976–77)

*Scope:* A catalog of 2,061 generally available free and free loan educational and informational guidance materials including 795 films, 83 filmstrips, 60 sets of slides, 453 audiotapes, 64 videotapes, 4 scripts, 211 audiodiscs, and 391 supplementary materials such as bulletins, pamphlets, study guides, handbooks, charts, posters, brochures, and books.

*Arrangement:* By type of medium followed by subject categories, then alphabetical by title.

*Entries:* Title, distributor/producer/publisher, author, date, length in number of minutes/frames/items/pages, speed, silent or sound, color or b/w, availability of scripts or phonodiscs to accompany filmstrips, limitations of distribution, descriptive annotation.

*Special Features:* Introduction gives directions for obtaining the material; source and availability index gives terms of loan and length of time necessary for bookings; television clearance; title index; detailed subject index; Australian availability index; Canadian availability index; sections of the *Guide* differentiated by use of colored paper.

74. **Educators Guide to Free Health, Physical Education and Recreation Materials,** compiled and edited by Foley A. Horkheimer. 9th ed. Edu-

cators Progress Service, Randolph, WI 53956. 1976. $11. 521p. Revised annually. (For use during the school year 1976–77)

*Scope:* A catalog of 2,484 generally available free and free loan educational and informational materials concerned with health, physical education, and recreation and including 1,363 films, 98 filmstrips, 101 sets of slides, 1 set of transparencies, 61 audiotapes, 78 videotapes, 6 scripts, 20 audiodiscs, 756 charts, exhibits, magazines, posters, and other printed media. Specific subjects included are: accident prevention and safety, career opportunities, diseases, handicaps, mental health, first aid, foods and nutrition, personal health, public health, sanitation and environmental control, sex education, family living, physical fitness, sports, indoor and outdoor activities.

*Arrangement:* By type of medium followed by subject categories, then alphabetical by title.

*Entries:* Title, distributor/producer/publisher, author, date, length in number of minutes/frames/slides/pages, speed, color or b/w, interest level, availability of script or sound accompaniment, silent or sound, limitations of distribution, descriptive annotation.

*Special Features:* Introduction gives general directions for obtaining the material; title index; detailed subject index; source and availability index gives terms of loan and length of time necessary for bookings, television clearance, and ability of distributor to fill requests; Australian availability index; Canadian availability index; sections of the *Guide* differentiated by use of colored paper.

75. **Educators Guide to Free Science Materials,** compiled and edited by Mary Horkheimer Saterstrom and John W. Renner. 17th ed. Educators Progress Service, Randolph, WI 53956. 1976. $11.25. 415p. Revised annually. (For use during the school year 1976–77)

*Scope:* A catalog of 1,822 generally available free and free loan educational and informational science materials including 992 films, 40 filmstrips, 36 slides, 1 set of transparencies, 160 audiotapes, 48 videotapes, 2 scripts, 5 transcriptions, and 538 supplementary materials, such as bulletins, pamphlets, exhibits, charts, posters, and books.

*Arrangement:* By type of medium followed by subject categories, then alphabetical by title.

*Entries:* Title, distributor/producer/publisher, author, date, length in number of minutes/frames/items/pages, color or b/w, availability of scripts or phonodiscs to accompany filmstrips, limitations of distribution, descriptive annotation.

*Special Features:* Introduction gives directions for obtaining the material; source and availability index gives terms of loan and length of time necessary for bookings; title index; detailed subject index; eight sample curriculum units demonstrate use of materials; Australian availability index; Canadian availability index; sections of the *Guide* differentiated by use of colored paper.

76. **Educators Guide to Free Social Studies Materials,** compiled and edited by Patricia H. Suttles and Steven A. Suttles with William H. Hartley. 16th ed. Educators Progress Service, Randolph, WI 53956. 1976. $11.75. 616p. Revised annually. (For use during the school year 1976–77)

*Scope:* A catalog of 3,902 generally available free and free loan educational and informational social studies materials including 1,555 films, 138 filmstrips, 136 sets of slides, 865 audiotapes, 102 videotapes, 8 scripts, 342 transcriptions, and 756 supplementary materials such as bulletins, pamphlets, exhibits, charts, posters, and books.

*Arrangement:* By type of medium followed by subject categories, then alphabetical by title.

*Entries:* Title, distributor/producer/publisher, author, date, length in number of minutes/frames/slides/pages, speed, color or b/w, interest level, availability of script or sound accompaniment, silent or sound, limitations of distribution, descriptive annotation.

*Special Features:* Introduction gives general directions for obtaining the material; title index; detailed subject index; source and availability index gives terms of loan and length of time necessary for bookings, television clearance, and ability of distributor to fill requests; Australian availability index; Canadian availability index; sections of the *Guide* differentiated by use of colored paper.

77. **Educators Guide to Free Tapes, Scripts, and Transcriptions,** compiled and edited by James L. Berger with Walter A. Wittich. 23rd ed. Educators Progress Service, Randolph, WI 53956. 1976. $10.50. 271p. Revised annually. (For use during the school year 1976–77)

*Scope:* A catalog of 1,636 titles of materials which are available on free loan to superintendents, audiovisual education directors, librarians, and teachers. Included are 246 videotapes, 1,022 audiotapes, 12 scripts, and 356 audiodiscs concerned with the following curriculum areas: guidance, health and physical education, home economics, language arts, science, and social studies.

*Arrangement:* By subject categories, then alphabetical by title.

*Entries:* Title, distributor, date, running time, speed (rpm or ips), availability, descriptive annotation.

*Special Features:* Source and availability index gives terms of loan
and length of time necessary for booking; title index; detailed subject index; Canadian availability index; sections of the *Guide* differentiated by the use of colored paper.

78. **EFLA Evaluations.** Educational Film Library Association, 43 W.
Sixty-first St., New York, NY 10023. Monthly. 1946 to date. Available
to members only; membership $50, $75, $100, $125 depending on size
of film library. 8½″ x 11½″ loose-leaf punched sheets, 8 evaluations
per page, 40 evaluations per month, 10 sets per year, *Cumulative Title
Index,* monthly *Subject Index,* and annual *Cumulative Subject Index.*
(Until December 1974 evaluations were issued on 3½″ x 5″ cards and
cumulated in the hard cover *Film Evaluation Guide 1946–1965,* now
out of print, and the *Supplement 1965–1967.* $12; *Supplement 1967–
1971.* $12. Future supplements planned)

*Scope:* Evaluations of 400 films per year in all instructional subjects
and for all age levels and types of audiences, provided by approximately 50 EFLA volunteer preview committees.
*Arrangement:* Alphabetical by title.
*Entries:* Title, length, color or b/w, rental/purchase price, date, director when known, producer, distributor, subject area, evaluator,
synopsis, uses, audience, technical rating, critical comments, general rating, EFLA number.
*Special Features:* Loose-leaf format; cumulative indexes.

79. **8mm Films in Medicine and Health Sciences,** compiled by Reba A.
Benschoter. 3d ed. Communications Division, College of Medicine,
University of Nebraska, 602 S. Forty-fourth Ave., Omaha, NE 68105.
Survey supported by Public Health Service and National Library of
Medicine. 1976. $8. 580p.

*Scope:* More than 4,100 entries of 8mm medical and health science
films produced both commercially and privately.
*Arrangement:* Alphabetical by title under 22 subject headings: anatomy, basic sciences, cancer, clinical medicine, dermatology, embry-
ology, first aid and safety, health services and education, hospital
food service, hospital housekeeping, hospital ward clerk training,
nursing, obstetrics, ophthalmology, patient education (adult), patient education (child), pharmacology, psychiatry and psychology,
radiology, rehabilitation, surgery, and technology (medical).
*Entries:* Title, producer, production date if available, production
credits, length, sound or silent, color or b/w, type of 8mm format,
educational author credits, 20–40 word content summary, distributor, price.

*Special Features:* Survey report summary; selected bibliography; title index; distributors' address listing; loose-leaf format.

80. **The Elementary School Library Collection: A Guide to Books and Other Media.** Phases 1–2–3. 10th ed. Phyllis Van Orden, General Editor. The Bro-Dart Foundation, 124 Church St., New Brunswick, NJ 08901. 1976. $29.95. 780p. Revised annually.

*Scope:* An annotated classified (Dewey Abridged edition) catalog of books and nonbook materials considered to be basic for any school library serving grades kindergarten through six. Included are 9,913 entries; 1,701 are nonbook media, 83 are periodicals, 200 are reference works, and 400 are professional-use items. The nonbook media are integrated with the listings of books and include charts, 8mm filmloops, filmstrips, maps, multimedia kits, recordings and cassettes, slides, study and art prints, and transparencies. Phase designations are defined as follows: phase 1, opening day collection; phase 2, for continuing development; phase 3, of specialized significance. Professional and audiovisual materials may receive any phase. The Spache formula is used for readability testing for books of first and second grade levels; the Fry graph is used for grades 3 through 6. The catalog is a continuing program with entries evaluated and reevaluated by a selection committee and its chairman, who is the general editor.

*Arrangement:* Main body—by Dewey Decimal Classification number; separate sections for fiction, easy, periodicals, professional tools, and reference.

*Entries:* Dewey Decimal Classification number, symbol denoting type of medium (nonprint), author or composer, title, edition, publisher/producer, distributor, date, series note, teacher's guide if available, grade level, price, illustrations, color or b/w, sound, length in number of pages/minutes/frames/sides/discs/items in set, diameter in inches, speed (rpm or ips), type of format (for 8mm items), subject headings, descriptive annotation, double symbol indicating reader interest or appeal and reading difficulty.

*Special Features:* Statement of selection policies; directory of publishers and distributors; classification principles and policies; outline of the Dewey Decimal Classification system; separate author, title, and subject indexes; a graded list of materials for nursery through 2.2 levels; a list of books for independent reading.

81. **The Encyclopaedia Cinematographica,** edited by G. Wolf, Institut fur den Wissenchaftlichen Film, Gottingen, West Germany. Available

from Director of the American Archive of Encyclopaedia Cinemato-graphica, Audio-Visual Services, 17 Willard Building, Pennsylvania State University, University Park, PA 16802. 1972. Free. 209p. *Supplement 1974–1975.* Free. 28p.; *Supplement 1976–1977.* Free. 15p.

*Scope:* More than 2,000 16mm scientific films (mostly silent) are in-dexed in the main volume and its supplements. Films have been submitted by scientists throughout the world and considered by an international board with headquarters in Germany to have a high degree of authenticity and scientific accuracy and to depict a single phenomenon or behavior which cannot be observed by the unaided human, which needs to be compared with other phenomena, which does not occur frequently, or which is disappearing from the cul-ture. Subjects include: zoology, physiology, invertebrata, verte-brata, amphibia, aves, mammalia, cytology, microbiology, ethnol-ogy, botany, social anthropology, folk life, technical sciences.

*Arrangement:* Alphabetical by title within broad subject areas.

*Entries:* Title (original language, English translation), date, color or b/w, sound if applicable, length, scientist, country of origin.

*Special Features:* Procedures for submitting scientific films; statutes of the organization; members of the Editorial Board; rental proce-dures for use within the United States.

82. **Energy Films Catalog.** Audiovisual Branch, Office of Public Affairs, U.S. Energy Research and Development Administration, Washington, DC 20545. 1976. Free. 71p.

*Scope:* A list of 188 titles available on free loan from the ERDA Film Library for educational nonprofit group use by schools, television stations, civic clubs, government and industrial organizations inter-ested in educational and informational films as well as technical and professional films on energy and energy related subjects. The films represent a number of producers and are for sale from several sources. The contents are fully described, including appropriate audience levels and honors received by the films.

*Arrangement:* By subject fields, then alphabetical by title.

*Entries:* File number, title, date, length in minutes, color or b/w, series title, audience level, description of content, television clear-ance, honors if any.

*Special Features:* About ERDA; catalog format and use; how to bor-row films; outline of subject headings; subject section—film titles in subject order; film titles in alphabetical order; film titles index—listing producers, sponsors, and sales sources; sales source ad-dresses; film mailing time map; photographic illustrations.

83. **Entelek Programmed Instruction Guide: Elementary/High School.**
3d ed. Entelek Inc., 42 Pleasant St., Newburyport, MA 01950. 1973.
$9.95. 287p. Also available, *Entelek Computer-Based Education Abstracts*, a quarterly service providing abstracts of CBE research and applications literature. 1965 to date. $77.50 annual subscription; $19.95 single issue.

*Scope:* More than 1,200 programs in all subject fields for grades K-12 are included in this revised edition of the *Guide*. The information is furnished to the Entelek data bank by 82 participating publishers who also write the descriptions of the programs.

*Arrangement:* By subject according to the Dewey Decimal Classification System.

*Entries:* Dewey Decimal number, serial number, title, author, publisher, date, level, target audience, description furnished by publisher, length in number of pages/frames/hours, components if any, prerequisites, objectives, tests, evaluation data given/not given, teaching devices required, cost, publisher's catalog number.

*Special Features:* Key to device code; brief listing by subject; listing by grade level; listing by publisher; listing by target population; addresses of publishers.

84. **The Environment Film Review: A Critical Guide to Ecology Films.**
Film Reference Department, Environment Information Center, Inc., 292 Madison Ave., New York, NY 10017. 1972. $20. 155p. Updated at 4-month intervals with citations to new films included in *Environment Abstracts*. Monthly. $200 per year.

*Scope:* A comprehensive selection of 627 films covering such areas of environmental affairs as: air pollution, chemical and biological contamination, energy, environmental education, environmental design and urban ecology, food and drugs, general, international, land use and misuse, noise pollution, nonrenewable resources, oceans and estuaries, population planning and control, radiological contamination, renewable resources—terrestrial, renewable resources—water, solid waste, transportation, water pollution, weather modification and geophysical change, wildlife. The annotations are descriptive and critical of the contents, treatment, and ecological objectivity of each film. Two stars are awarded to films with superior cinematic treatment and subject coverage; films with either of the above, or a bit of both, received one star.

*Arrangement:* Review section—alphabetical by categories listed above, then numerically by film accession number.

*Entries:* Star rating when appropriate, accession number, title, length in minutes, color or b/w, free loan or purchase/rental prices, release date, sponsor when given, producer and/or distributor, director/writer/narrator whenever significant, intended audience, descriptive-critical review, cross reference to other reviews when appropriate.

*Special Features:* Alphabetical title index with complete citations for all films; key word list; subject index; industry index; sponsor index; standard abbreviations.

85. **Family Life: Literature and Films: An Annotated Bibliography.** Minnesota Council on Family Relations, 1219 University Ave., Minneapolis, MN 55414. 1972. $7 postpaid. 353p. *Supplement.* 1974. $7 postpaid. 235p. $12.75 postpaid for both volumes. Available also in microfiche and hard copy from ERIC Document Reproduction Service, P.O. Box 190, Arlington, VA 22210. Apply for current prices. ED 118 234. *Supplement.* ED 118 235.

*Scope:* Two extensive bibliographies of books, curriculum guides, periodicals, films, filmstrips, records, tapes, and multimedia kits mainly intended for professional and lay persons. Some references for children and adolescents are included. The selections were made by a review panel and include the following broad subjects: the family, female and male roles, sexuality and sex education, human reproduction and family planning, adolescence and youth, looking toward marriage, marital interaction, family crises, child development and parenthood, middle and later years, self-growth, social issues and the family, family life education. Descriptive annotations and notes under subject headings suggest uses and audience levels.

*Arrangement:* By broad subjects in the order listed above, subdivided by specific subjects, then by type of medium.

*Entries:* Author (for print materials), title or series titles, publisher/producer, distributor, date, length in pages/minutes/frames, price (except for films), color or b/w, individual titles in series or set, descriptive annotation.

*Special Features:* Publishers and sources; periodicals; audiovisual producers and distributors; author index.

86. **Feature Films on 8mm and 16mm: A Directory of Feature Films Available for Rental, Sale, and Lease in the United States,** edited by James L. Limbacher. 4th ed. R. R. Bowker Co., 1180 Avenue of the Americas, New York, NY 10036. 1974. $16.50. 400p.

*Scope:* More than 15,000 entries are included in this updated reference and booking source. All are currently available in the United States regardless of where in the world they were produced and range from early silent classics through 1973 releases. Documentaries, animated cartoons, and films with no professional casts are also included.

*Arrangement:* Alphabetical by title.

*Entries:* Title, date, names of stars, running time, distributor, type (feature, documentary, or animated cartoon), color or b/w, country, technical information.

*Special Features:* A geographical index to film distributors; an index to directors; an index to film serials.

87. **Film as an Aid to Archaeological Teaching,** compiled by Marion du Moulin. The Archaeological Institute of America, 260 W. Broadway, New York, NY 10013. 1972. $1.50. 35p.

*Scope:* An annotated list of more than 100 16mm films considered to be of use to teachers engaged in archaeology and possibly of some help to those in related fields such as art history and anthropology. Grade levels range from intermediate through college with some films suitable also for use by clubs and societies for more advanced audiences.

*Arrangement:* Alphabetical by title.

*Entries:* Title, running time, color or b/w, rental price, age level, distributor, descriptive annotation.

*Special Features:* Subject index; names and addresses of distributors; publications available from the Archaeological Institute of America.

88. **A Film Guide on China,** edited by Christopher J. Wiley. Southern California Field Staff of the National Committee on United States-China Relations, Inc., 1119 Campbell Hall, University of California, Los Angeles, CA 90024. Available in microfiche and hard copy from ERIC Document Reproduction Service, P.O. Box 190, Arlington, VA 22210. 1974. Apply for current prices. 27p. ED 111 756.

*Scope:* A list of 81 16mm films on China with descriptive/evaluative reviews taken from publications of the National Committee and from the film catalogs published by the Los Angeles Public Library, local universities, and film companies.

*Arrangement:* By categories—China before 1949, China after 1949, Taiwan, Chinese culture—then alphabetical by title.

*Entries:* Title, length, color or b/w, date, intended audience, rental source, catalog number if any, rental price, evaluative annotation, asterisk denoting titles of better quality.

*Special Features:* Audiotapes of interviews and panel discussions by leading China scholars—on free loan from the Southern California Field Staff tape library; directory of field staffs in other states; brief information on the National Committee and on the Southern California Field Staff; terms and rates of rental sources.

89. **Film Music: From Violins to Video,** by James L. Limbacher. Scarecrow Press, P.O. Box 656, Metuchen, NJ 08840. 1974. $18.50. 835p. (Supersedes *A Selected List of Recorded Musical Scores from Radio, Television, and Motion Pictures*)

*Scope:* The book is divided into two parts: part 1 consists of nine chapters (191 pages) of articles about the history, techniques, and characteristics of film music; the articles are written by authorities in the field and are reprinted from music periodicals. Part 2 lists films, dates, composers, and recorded musical scores, in four chapters, each arranged differently to provide access to the information by each of the above components.

*Arrangement:* In two parts as described above. The opening section of part 2, "Film Titles and Dates," lists all titles in the volume alphabetically and serves as an index to the second section "Films and their Composers," in which all titles are listed by year of release together with name(s) of composer(s) or musical director(s). The third section, "Composers and their Films," is also arranged by year of release, then alphabetically by composers/directors, followed by film titles credited to them, in alphabetical order. The fourth section, "Recorded Musical Scores," lists most of the known musical scores for films which have been recorded on discs or tapes for commercial use. "Musical movies which feature a song score are seldom included" (Chapter 12).

*Entries:* Film title, year of release, title source (producer, studio, country, etc.) in code, composer, musical director, producer label and number. (Order and inclusion of these components varies in each chapter.)

*Special Features:* Index to Part 1.

90. **Film News Omnibus,** edited by Rohama Lee. Film News, 250 W. Fifty-seventh St., New York, NY 10019. 1973. $17.50 if billed; $15 if check accompanies order. 270p. (A second volume including 1973 through 1975 reviews is scheduled for publication in late 1976)

*Scope:* Objective, professional reviews of 42 feature films and 450 documentaries and short subjects which appeared originally over a three-year period, 1970–72, in *Film News* magazine. Some of the films date back to the silent film era; some have won awards and prizes. Annotations include a description of content and a critical review along with suggestions about appropriate audiences and uses.

*Arrangement:* Alphabetical by title in two categories: feature films; documentaries and short subjects.

*Entries:* Title, date, length in minutes, color or b/w, producer/distributor, free loan or rental/sales prices, prizes if any, description of content and signed review.

*Special Features:* Title and subject indexes; reviewers and their credentials; directory of producers/distributors in the United States and Canada; illustrations from the films; two introductory articles— "The Feature Film in 16mm" and "The Documentary and Short Subject."

91. **Film Programmer's Guide to 16mm Rentals,** compiled and edited by Kathleen Weaver. 2d ed. Reel Research, Box 6037, Albany, CA 94706. 1975. $9 postpaid to individuals; $11 postpaid to institutions. 212p.

*Scope:* A list of approximately 10,000 rental titles of feature films available in 16mm format from 60 U.S. distributors. Designed to provide convenient access to a wide range of films, "the *Guide* is particularly geared to reflect the expanding interest in the history of cinema, in underground and experimental films, and in social and political documentaries. At the same time it includes the standard repertory of Hollywood features and foreign classics" (Introduction). Rental information was obtained from the distributors' catalogs, with reference to *The World Encyclopedia of the Film*. Educational films are not included.

*Arrangement:* In 3 sections—main title directory, documentaries, and newsreels—all alphabetical by title.

*Entries:* Title, director, date, sound or silent, length, color or b/w, distributor (code), rental price.

*Special Features:* Selected directors' index; early cinema (1890–1915); distributors' rental information.

92. **Film Resources for Sex Education.** Sex Information and Education Council of the U.S. (SIECUS), 137 N. Franklin Ave., Hempstead, NY 11550. Distributed by Human Sciences Press, 72 Fifth Ave., New York, NY 10011. 1976. Apply. 52p.

*Scope:* An annotated list of 16mm films, filmstrips, slides, cassettes, and transparencies which have been reviewed either by SIECUS Editorial Staff or by members of the SIECUS Board of Directors. The reviews originally appeared in the *SIECUS Newsletter,* volumes 1 to 7, and volumes 1 through 3 of the *SIECUS Report.* "Inclusion of a film in this guide does not constitute endorsement by SIECUS; it is an indication that the reviewers have found, through experience, that the material can be used effectively in an educational setting" (Introduction).

*Arrangement:* Alphabetical by title.

*Entries:* Title or series title, date, type of medium, color or b/w, sound or captioned, length in minutes/items/frames, accompanying materials/guide if any, descriptive-evaluative annotation, audience level, individual titles if a series, distributor, purchase and rental prices.

*Special Features:* Subject and audience level index; distributors with addresses.

93. **Film Resources on Japan,** prepared by the Audio-Visual Center, University of Michigan, Ann Arbor, pursuant to a contract with the Office of Education, U.S. Department of Health, Education, and Welfare. Available from the Superintendent of Documents, U.S. Government Printing Office, Washington, DC 20402. 1975. $1.20. 55p.

*Scope:* A comprehensive list of 355 films (16mm) and 204 filmstrips assumed to have utility in the study of Japan. "Inclusion of a title in this directory is not a recommendation for use for any instructional purpose, and no attempt has been made to include detailed or critical evaluations of the materials listed or described. Schools are advised to use this handbook as a means of locating promising material, a first step in selection . . ." (Notes). The descriptive list of films includes only those titles produced after 1960, but there is a list of 37 older titles (without annotations) which may still be useful. Also includes without annotations a list of "sponsored" films and a list of 35mm filmstrips. Main subjects are: agriculture, animal life, anthropology, architecture, art, atomic energy, business, children, climate, communism, customs/traditions, economics, education, energy, engineering, environment, family life, festivals, fishing, flowers, folklore, food, geography, government, handicrafts, history, industry, international relations, Japanese-American relations, judo, karate, Kyoto, language arts, music, natural resources, performing arts, philosophy, physical education, poetry, political science, religion, rice, rural life, silk, sports, stories, Tokyo, transportation, urban life, women.

*Arrangement:* The first section is a subject index with film titles listed alphabetically under the subjects; the second section is an annotated list of 16mm motion pictures, arranged alphabetically by title; remaining sections—Films Produced before 1960, "Sponsored" Films, and 35mm Filmstrips—are arranged alphabetically by title.

*Entries:* Film entries in the descriptive list include title, running time, color or b/w, grade level, content description, producer and/or distributor, year of production; entries for "Sponsored" films and older films include title, running time, color or b/w, distributor, and dates (for the films produced before 1960); filmstrip entries include title, number of frames, color or b/w, sound if any, appropriate levels of use, distributor code, and production date.

*Special Features:* List of distributors with addresses.

94. **Film Reviews in Psychiatry, Psychology and Mental Health: A Descriptive and Evaluative Listing of Educational and Instructional Films,** edited by Robert E. Froelich. Pierian Press, 5000 Washtenaw Ave., Ann Arbor, MI 48104. 1974. $9.95. 142p.

*Scope:* Descriptive-critical reviews of 123 teaching films. The reviews were written by medical authorities and members of the film review board of the American Psychiatric Association who previewed and evaluated the films over a period of several years. The foreword includes a discussion of the "state of the art" and suggestions for using films in teaching. Some of the many subjects dealt with in the films are: anger, child hospitalization, community psychiatry, depression, development, drug therapy, growth, hospitalization, interview, mother child relationship, neurologic examination, police, psychosomatic, recreation, research, social issues, and treatment.

*Arrangement:* Alphabetical by title.

*Entries:* Title, length in minutes, sound or silent, color or b/w, date, description of content, critical comments, suggested audience and uses, reviewer(s), producer/author/editor/consultant, distributor code.

*Special Features:* Index of additional reviews of these titles; index of reviewers; tabular cross-index of reviews and reviewers, audience, and type of film; index of medical consultants and/or authors; distributor index; subject index.

95. **A Filmography for American Indian Education,** prepared by Carroll Warner Williams and Gloria Bird, with the support of the Research and Cultural Studies Development Section, Santa Fe Bureau of Indian Affairs, U.S. Department of Interior. Distributed by Zia Cine, Inc., P.O. Box 493, Santa Fe, NM 87501. 1973. $5. 192p. Available also in microfiche only from ERIC Document Reproduction Service, P.O. Box 190, Arlington, VA 22210. Apply for current price. ED 091 101.

*Scope:* A descriptive list of approximately 550 films on native Americans in the Western hemisphere. In compiling the list, all film distributors in the United States and all institutions engaged in Indian education were requested to send information about available films.

In addition, more than 2,300 questionnaires concerning Indian education films and film use were sent to Indian and non-Indian leaders from education, anthropology, educational film, sociology, and psychology. Almost all possible films were then screened, most of them by an Indian audience for criticism and review. Over 300 reviews were written and collected. In addition to details about the procedure in compiling the catalog, the introduction discusses the types of films and suggests ways to use them in the classroom.

*Arrangement:* Alphabetical by title.

*Entries:* Title, length, color or b/w, sound or silent, size in mm, distributor code, rental/sale price, description of content.

*Special Features:* Entries too late for cataloging; Bureau of Indian Affairs films; distributors; title index.

96. **A Filmography of Films about Movies and Movie Making** (T–26). Eastman Kodak Co., Department 454, Rochester, NY 14650. 1974. 10 for $7.20; 100 for $53.30. 18p. (Revision scheduled for late 1977)

*Scope:* A major revision of a work originally compiled by Robert W. Wagner and David L. Parker, published by Eastman in 1969 and revised in 1971 and 1974. The current edition includes 300 titles— 67 more than the preceding edition. New titles have been added and some older titles have been eliminated because the films have been withdrawn by their distributors. Included are films illustrating various aspects of motion picture production, the history of cinema, facts about motion picture film, and the nature of the medium. Films are 16mm or 8mm, color or black and white sound films unless otherwise noted.

*Arrangement:* Alphabetical by title.

*Entries:* Title, date, producer and/or distributor, running time, brief description of content in 10–50 words.

*Special Features:* An alphabetical listing of sources of films about movies and movie making, with addresses.

97. **Filmography of the African Humanities,** prepared by Steven Feld and the African Studies Program, Indiana University, Woodburn Hall, Room 223, Bloomington, IN 47401. 1972. $1.00. 54p. Supply limited.

*Scope:* A total of 223 films that deal wholly or in large part with the African humanities and which constitute the bulk of the motion pictures available in 1972 in the fields of dance, arts and crafts, music, drama, folklore, and literature. The list is not exhaustive inasmuch as sufficient documentation could not be obtained for some recent French ethnographic films.

*Arrangement:* Alphabetical by title.

*Entries:* Title, location, length, color or b/w, sound or silent, language of the commentary, producer, distributor code, one-sentence synopsis.

*Special Features:* Indexes to dance films, music films, visual arts and crafts films, drama, folklore, and literature films; index of distributors.

98. **A Filmography of the Third World: An Annotated List of 16mm Films,** by Helen W. Cyr. Scarecrow Press, Inc., Box 656, Metuchen, NJ 08840. 1976. $11. 319p.

*Scope:* "Third world," as defined by the author of this selected, annotated list, includes all non-Western nations—that is, all except the United States, Europe, and the Soviet Union—and the ethnic minorities of North America and Europe. Approximately 2,000 titles ranging from short to feature-length films are included covering such subjects as customs, geographic features, history, science, politics, fine arts, religion, sports, technology, and travel; fictional films are listed also. A majority of the films were released during the late 1960s or the 1970s. Gaps were filled with "older films which can at least illustrate geographic features or the sociology, anthropology, or politics of former years" (Introduction). Deliberately added are "old films that are critically acclaimed classics of ageless appeal and importance." Excluded are films which exploit a popular theme or "which demonstrate reverse stereotyping." Inclusion in the list does not constitute the author's endorsement of a film's content or point of view.

*Arrangement:* Alphabetical by geographic areas and nations, then alphabetical by title.

*Entries:* Title, alternate title if any, production company/producer/ filmmaker, release or copyright date, series title, running time, color or b/w, code(s) for distributor(s), brief descriptive annotation. Additional data for feature-length theatrical films: foreign language, English subtitles if any, director, credits, and cast.

*Special Features:* Film distributors; list of directors, cinematographers, scenarists, and composers; index of film titles.

99. **Films and Filmstrips on Early Childhood,** compiled by Lillian Canzler, Washington Center for Early Childhood Education, Central Washington State College. Available from the CWSC Bookstore, Ellensburg, WA 98926. 1974. $4.62 paper. 71p. Available also in microfiche and hard copy from ERIC Document Reproduction Service, P.O. Box 190, Arlington, VA 22210. ED 113 036.

*Scope:* The films and filmstrips in this bibliography are concerned
with the following categories of early childhood education: child
development, community and parent education, culture and children, current trends in early childhood education, curriculum, and
teacher training. The entries were considered on the basis of
aesthetics, content, and technical quality; most are rated with the
Winick rating system of one, two, three, or four stars. In some cases,
films have not been rated which means that they have not been
previewed.

*Arrangement:* In six categories mentioned above, then alphabetical
by title.

*Entries:* Title, running time, color or b/w, purchase or rental price,
distributor, description of content with rating, producer, year of
release.

*Special Features:* Film title index; sources consulted. Many of the
entries in this list as well as the rating scale are from *Films for
Early Childhood: A Selected Annotated Bibliography,* by Mariann
Pezzela Winick (see entry no.105) and are included with the
author's permission.

100. **Films & Filmstrips on Legal & Law-Related Subjects: A Listing
with Sources,** compiled by the Audio-Visual Department, Division
of Communications, American Bar Association, 1155 E. Sixtieth St.,
Chicago, IL 60637. 1974. Apply. 82p.

*Scope:* A comprehensive catalog of films and filmstrips on the law
and our legal system, "representing most of the major works on
these subjects produced during the past 20 years" (General Information, p.1). The purpose of the compilation is to identify visual
aids that explain the American concept of law and justice, that
help educate citizens to their legal rights and responsibilities and
which offer continuing legal education to practicing lawyers.
More than 800 titles are listed in this greatly expanded revised
edition to which filmstrips are included for the first time. The 20
subject categories are: biographical, civil rights/individual rights/
women's rights, communism, constitution/Bill of Rights, consumer
protection/education, corrections/prison reform, courts/judicial
process, crime, domestic relations/marriage and divorce, drug
abuse/alcoholism, government/citizenship, law-related historical
events, international law, juvenile delinquency, law enforcement
legal profession, law (specialized), medicine and the law, military
justice, social and contemporary issues, traffic courts. The films
and filmstrips listed have not been screened by the American Bar
Association and should not be interpreted as having ABA approval.

*Arrangement:* Alphabetical by title under the above-mentioned subject headings and subheadings. The opening section of the catalog is a category index with titles listed under subject and a reference to the page which contains the full description of the work.

*Entries:* Title or series title, audience level in code, title number for use in ordering, description of content, date if available, length, color or b/w, rental/purchase price, producer when available, distributor.

*Special Feature:* Film/filmstrip distributors.

101. **Films and Filmstrips on Occupational Safety and Health.** National Institute for Occupational Safety and Health, Center for Disease Control, Public Health Service, U.S. Department of Health, Education, and Welfare. Available from the Superintendent of Documents, U.S. Government Printing Office, Washington, DC 20402. 1975. $1.10. 51p. (Publication no.NIOSH 75–128) Cover title: *NIOSH Films and Filmstrips on Occupational Safety and Health.*

*Scope:* A list of 228 free loan films and filmstrips available from U.S. government agencies and various commercial sources. Major subjects include: chemicals, construction and plant safety, electricity, eyes and vision, fire and explosion, general safety, hospitals and nursing, industrial hygiene, industrial medicine, laboratory safety, lead, mercury, mining, noise, pesticides, power tools, protective devices, radiation, skin, supervision.

*Arrangement:* First section is an alphabetical index of subjects with titles listed alphabetically under each subject. Main body is arranged alphabetically by title.

*Entries:* Title, type of medium, sound or silent, color or b/w, date if available, brief descriptive annotation, name and address of source.

*Special Features:* List of organizations providing rental or sale films and filmstrips dealing with occupational safety and health; addresses of local army area headquarters.

102. **Films by and/or about Women 1972, A Directory of Filmmakers, Films, and Distributors: Internationally, Past and Present.** Women's History Research Center, Inc., 2325 Oak St., Berkeley, CA 94708. 1972. $3 to individual women; $5 to groups and institutions; 50¢ shipping and handling; prepaid or vouchered orders only. 72p.

*Scope:* The films in this directory come from several sources: (1) films by women on any subject; (2) films by men or organizations which illustrate something a women's group has wanted to communicate about women; (3) films by men about a particular woman or women's event. The films are grouped into categories, some of which designate the style or type of production, e.g., animated, documentaries, experimental, avant-garde, classics. Other categories are subjects: birth control, careers and job discrimination, child care, marriage, female biographies, female liberation movement, performing arts, sensuality—sexuality, social protest, and third world. With some exceptions, the descriptions of the films are written by the filmmaker or distributor.

*Arrangement:* Alphabetical by title under subject or film-type category.

*Entries:* Title, length, size (mm), color or b/w, rental and/or sale price, filmmaker, source, brief description.

*Special Features:* Index of films by female filmmakers; index of films by distributors; films in progress; last minute additions.

103. **Films for Anthropological Teaching,** by Karl G. Heider. 5th ed. Distributed by the American Anthropological Association, 1703 New Hampshire Ave., N.W., Washington, DC 20009. 1972. $3 to individuals; $5 to institutions. 69p.

*Scope:* The purpose of this comprehensive catalog "is to facilitate the use of the film as a source of information" (Introduction). Topics included are: archaeology, art, change/modernization, economics/ecology, ethnology, field work, paralinguistics, ritual, social conflict and resolution, social organization and kinship, technology. The geographical areas represented are: Africa, Near East, Asia, Europe, Middle America, Caribbean, South America, North America, and Oceania. This fifth edition contains approximately 420 titles, an increase of about 60 percent over the fourth edition of 2 years ago.

*Arrangement:* Alphabetical by title.

*Entries:* Title, date, running time, director, producer, anthropologist, cameraman/photographer, consultant, writer, editor, narrator, music, sound recordist, distributor and order number, rental/sales price, descriptive annotation, bibliographic entries for reviews of the film, related films or publications.

*Special Features:* Index of films by geographical areas; index of films by topics; author index; distributor index; introductory discussion of sources and of appropriate film uses; description of the *Encyclopaedia Cinematographica.*

104. **Films for Children: A Selected List,** prepared by the Children's and Young Adult Services Section, New York Library Association. 3d ed. Available from the New York Library Association, 60 E. Forty-second St., Suite 1242, New York, NY 10017. 1972. $3 prepaid. 32p.

*Scope:* More than 200 highly selected films which children have enjoyed over a period of years, and which represent a wide range of subjects. In general, the selection committee did not include classroom films except where factual material was presented in an imaginative, artistic way, e.g., Walt Disney's *Secrets of the Bee World*. The introduction includes the criteria for selection, cites reviewing services, and offers practical suggestions for planning, projecting, and staging the film program.

*Arrangement:* Alphabetical by title with a subject index.

*Entries:* Title, length, color or b/w, purchase price, audience level, descriptive annotation (except for titles included in the 1969 edition or those well known), distributor, date.

*Special Features:* Sample multimedia program; directory of distributors.

105. **Films for Early Childhood: A Selected Annotated Bibliography,** by Mariann Pezzella Winick. Early Childhood Education Council of New York City. Available from Sylvia Shapiro, ECEC Publications, 32–16 One Hundred and Sixty-sixth St., Flushing, NY 11358. 1973. $3.50; 5 copies or more $3 each. 125p.

*Scope:* Critical evaluations and descriptions of more than 250 films for use in teacher education, staff workshops, parent and community meetings. Films are rated "adequate" to "excellent" on a one- to four-star scale and are grouped in the following categories: development, current trends, program planning, curriculum, parent education, community education, comparative education, special education, children, teacher training, titles of series.

*Arrangement:* By categories in the order listed above, then alphabetical by title.

*Entries:* Title or series title followed by individual titles, length, color or b/w, purchase and rental prices, producer, distributor and/or rental source, rating, evaluative annotation.

*Special Features:* List of distributors and producers with addresses; title index.

106. **Films for Special Education,** by John L. Tringo. New England Special Education Instructional Materials Center, Boston University, Boston, MA 02215. Available in microfiche and hard copy from ERIC Document Reproduction Service, P.O. Box 190, Arlington, VA 22210. 1972. Apply for current prices. 102p. ED 079 887.

*Scope:* A comprehensive list of 500 films available for teachers, clinicians, parents, and others concerned with the education of handicapped children. The list was compiled from film company catalogs, social agency lists, and the catalog of the National Audio-visual Center. The subjects and number of films in each category are: adult-child relationships (27), behavior modification (10), blind and partially sighted (31), child development (15), crippled and neurologically impaired (25), deaf and hard of hearing (25), early education (12), educable mentally retarded (8), emotionally disturbed and socially maladjusted (64), general special education (35), gifted (7), learning disabilities (48), mentally retarded (59), multiple handicapped (6), orthopedically handicapped (13), physical education (8), psychological testing (7), severely mentally retarded (19), speech impaired (45), teacher training and techniques (34). The films are described but not evaluated.

*Arrangement:* Alphabetical by subjects listed above, then alphabetical by title.

*Entries:* Title, series title, running time, color or b/w, free loan/rental/purchase prices, sound or silent, name and address of distributor, description of content.

*Special Features:* Suggested sources for special education films; Instructional Materials Centers (IMC) location guide.

*Author's Note:* The IMCs mentioned directly above have been disbanded. On September 1, 1974, a restructured program of media and support services was initiated by the Bureau of Education for the Handicapped, Learning Resources Branch (BEH/LRB). The National Center on Educational Media and Materials for the Handicapped (NCEMMH) located at Ohio State University, 220 W. Twelfth Ave., Columbus, OH 43210, is a major unit within the learning resources program. In addition to NCEMMH, there are 4 Specialized Offices (SOs) and 13 Area Learning Resource Centers (ALRCs). The national and regional programs of these agencies are referred to collectively as the ALRC/SO/NCEMMH network which interfaces with state and local media-materials programs.

107. **Films in Children's Programs,** compiled by the Film Committee, Children's and Young People's Section, Wisconsin Library Association. Rev. ed. 201 W. Mifflin St., Madison, WI 53703. 1975. $2. 17p. (A continuation of lists with the same title prepared in 1969, 1970, and 1972)

*Scope:* An annotated list of 86 children's films which the committee previewed during the period beginning January 1974 through August 1975. The main section of the bibliography lists 43 titles suitable for use with children in grades 3 through 6. Suggested programming ideas and related materials are included in the annotations for these films as an aid in planning children's programs. The second section of the list includes 43 titles which were previewed but not selected for inclusion because of poor quality or because the films did not fit the age range or were for a very special audience.

*Arrangement:* In each section, alphabetical by title.

*Entries:* Title, length, color or b/w, producer/distributor, date, purchase and rental prices, descriptive/critical annotation.

*Special Features:* Directory of Film Distributors and Rental Sources.

108. **Films in Early Childhood Education,** compiled by Gary Cooke. Available in microfiche and hard cover from ERIC Document Reproduction Service, P.O. Box 190, Arlington, VA 22210. 1972. Apply for current prices. 29p. ED 075 069.

*Scope:* An annotated list of films on child development and on the various approaches to early childhood education. Some of the films are for use with children in the classroom, others are intended as guides and resource material for teachers. Evaluations are not included.

*Arrangement:* Alphabetical by title.

*Entries:* Title, date, color or b/w, running time, description, producer/distributor code, availability of handbook/guide.

*Special Features:* Film distributors.

109. **Films in Mental Retardation: A Selected Annotated Bibliography,** by Kevin McGovern and Esther B. Brummer. Rehabilitation Research and Training Center in Mental Retardation, Center for Human Development, College of Education, University of Oregon, Eugene, OR 97401. Available in microfiche and hard copy from ERIC Document Reproduction Service, P.O. Box 190, Arlington, VA 22210. 1973. Apply for current prices. 41p. ED 109 833.

*Scope:* An annotated list of 33 16mm films which have been previewed and/or used by the training staff of the Rehabilitation Research and Training Center in Mental Retardation. Subjects included are: treatment strategies, programs, attitudes, concepts, or theories related to rehabilitation of the retarded.

*Arrangement:* Alphabetical by title.

*Entries:* Title, color or b/w, running time, description of content, uses and suggested audience, reference to distributor.

*Special Features:* Film distributors; subject index.

110. **Films Kids Like: A Catalog of Short Films for Children,** compiled and edited by Susan Rice, assisted by Barbara Ludlum. Published for Center for Understanding Media, Inc., by the American Library Association, 50 E. Huron St., Chicago, IL 60611. 1973. $5.50. 150p.

*Scope:* An annotated list of approximately 225 short 16mm films which were viewed by children during a project conducted by the Children's Film Theater in New York. The primary interest of the staff was to compile a list of "films children liked, based on observed feelings and responses of children themselves—a listing that could be shared with teachers, librarians, and community people" (p.10).

*Arrangement:* Alphabetical by title.

*Entries:* Title, a one-paragraph descriptive/evaluative annotation, sound or silent, animation or live action, length, color or b/w, distributor code.

*Special Features:* Introduction describing the procedures followed and offering suggestions for establishing a children's film program; list of distributors with addresses; photographs of children engaged in project activities, photographs from the films, and reproductions of the children's art work.

111. **Films of a Changing World: A Critical International Guide,** by Jean Marie Ackermann. Society for International Development, 1346 Connecticut Ave., N.W., Washington, DC 20036. 1972. $4 prepaid; $3.50 each for 5 or more copies. 106p. (A continuation, *Films of a Changing World 1972–1976,* is scheduled for publication in late 1976)

*Scope:* A collection of 36 of the author's commentaries which critically review 222 development-oriented films about countries in Africa, Asia, Europe, Latin America, and a few about Canada and the United States. The reviews first appeared in the *International Development Review* during the period from March 1963 through December 1971 and are reprinted in this separate publication with the permission of the journal.

*Arrangement:* Individual films are grouped according to broad topics, described, and evaluated in 36 critical commentaries which are written in literary and narrative style. Bibliographical data for films and printed sources of information about films follow each commentary.

*Entries:* Title, length, color or b/w, date, producer/distributor with addresses, sales and rental prices when available.

*Special Features:* Alphabetical title index; geographical index; subject index; films and other media classified by subject; a sampling of catalogs, selected readings and references; selected periodicals.

112. **Films on Africa: An Educators Guide to 16mm Films Available in the Midwest,** compiled by the African Studies Program, University

of Wisconsin–Madison, 1450 Van Hise Hall, 1220 Linden Dr., Madison, WI 53706. December, 1974. Apply. 68p.

*Scope:* A catalog of all of the known 16mm films about Africa currently available from nonprofit educational and religious as well as commercial distributors in the Midwest. Films which are available only from distributors outside the Midwest are included also; these are primarily from African embassies and U.N. missions. The list is deliberately comprehensive, including both documentary and feature films as well as those of both very high and very low quality, those that are politically biased or highly stereotypical—"believing that teachers may even use bad films to illustrate political orientations and conflicts in Africa" (Introduction). In addition to the comprehensive annotated list, there is an initial chapter which lists by title (only) those films which other Africanists find useful in their teaching and those which they do not recommend due to age, bias, technical problems, or superficiality.

*Arrangement:* Alphabetical by title.

*Entries:* Title, date if available, length, color or b/w, sound or silent, audience or grade level, distributor code, rental and purchase prices, descriptive annotation from distributor's catalog.

*Special Features:* Directory of distributors arranged by states; additional sources of information about African film.

113. **Films on Death and Dying,** by Edward A. Mason. Educational Film Library Association, 43 W. Sixty-first St., New York, NY 10023. 1973. 75¢ prepaid. 4p. (EFLA Service Supplement)

*Scope:* A discursive list of 32 films for various age groups, compiled and critically evaluated by the Director of the Mental Health Training Film Program, Department of Psychiatry, Harvard Medical School. "The filmography tries to recognize the varied interests of audiences approaching this subject, but is far from definitive . . . among these titles there are films which can inspire and inform, films for training or entertainment, films which stand by themselves and those which ought to be followed by discussion" (p.1). Six titles "not yet reviewed" are listed at the end.

*Arrangement:* Alphabetical by title.

*Entries:* Title, length, color or b/w, date, rental/purchase price, distributor's name and address.

114. **Films—Too Good for Words: A Directory of Nonnarrated 16mm Films,** by Salvatore J. Parlato, Jr. R. R. Bowker Co., 1180 Avenue of the Americas, New York, NY 10036. 1973. $13. 209p.

*Scope:* Approximately 1,000 curriculum-oriented 16mm films that entertain as well as instruct students from elementary to adult education levels. While the films are without narration, they are not soundless; they use "music for the sake of mood, ambient noise for realism, and artificial sound for special effects" (Preface). Main subject categories are: arts, other places/other customs, science, nature, expression, city and suburb, values, fun, action, war and peace, fantasy, literature, and "more"—a category which includes a potpourri of subjects.

*Arrangement:* Divided into the 13 categories listed above, then alphabetical by title.

*Entries:* Title, factual one-paragraph annotation, awards if any, producer, distributor, length, color or b/w, sound or silent, date if available.

*Special Features:* Films indexed by title; films indexed by subject; producer/distributor directory.

115. **George Gershwin: A Selective Bibliography and Discography,** by Charles Schwartz. Published for The College Music Society by Information Coordinators, 1435–37 Randolph St., Detroit, MI 48226. 1974. $8.50. 118p. (Bibliographies in American Music, no.1)

*Scope:* In addition to an extensive discography of long-playing records of George Gershwin's concert and operatic works, collections of songs, musicals, and movies, the volume includes a list of the highlights of the composer's life and a selective bibliography of works about him. The discography includes a few key 78 rpm records which are now collectors items.

*Arrangement:* Divided into the sections mentioned above. The bibliography is arranged alphabetically by author; the highlights are listed chronologically; the discography is arranged by title or album title.

*Entries:* Title or album title, date, record label and number, performer or performing group, conductor, individual titles (in collections), an asterisk denoting 78 rpm, two asterisks denoting older LP, a plus ( + ) for recordings especially recommended.

*Special Features:* Portrait of George Gershwin, by Grancel Fitz.

116. **The Growing Years: A Bibliography of Affective Materials for the Preschool Child,** by Jackie Bolen. California Learning Resource Center, 600 S. Commonwealth Ave., Suite 1304, Los Angeles, CA 90005. Available in microfiche and hard copy from ERIC Document Reproduction Service, P.O. 190, Arlington, VA 22210. 1972. Apply for current prices. 38p. ED 078 618.

*Scope:* A list of approximately 90 multimedia kits, books, films, film-loops, filmstrips, records, cassettes, tapes, transparencies, professional materials, and picture story sets selected and evaluated in terms of their usefulness in developing affective behavior in normal and abnormal preschool children. A majority of the entries are children's books and filmstrips with records or cassettes.

*Arrangement:* By type of medium, then by publisher code number.

*Entries:* Publisher code number, album/series title, author, length in minutes/number of items, individual titles if a series, color or b/w, purchase/rental prices, description of content.

*Special Features:* List of publishers/producers; subject category index; "Newer News" (items located since the completion of the publication); bibliography of professional materials.

117. **Guide to Audiovisual Aids for Spanish-Speaking Americans: Health-Related Films, Filmstrips and Slides, Descriptions and Sources.** Health Services Administration, Public Health Service, U.S. Department of Health, Education, and Welfare, 5600 Fishers Lane, Rockville, MD 20852. 1973. Free. 37p. (DHEW Publication no.HSA 74–30). (A follow-up to *Spanish-Language Health Communication Teaching Aids,* DHEW Publication no.HSM 73–19, 1972)

*Scope:* The materials listed in this guide are distributed by universities, government agencies, professional associations, and commercial firms and may be obtained with Spanish-language soundtracks unless otherwise indicated. None of the materials has been previewed by members of the staff and the descriptive annotations are those of the distributors. Subjects included are: accident prevention, aging, community health, dental health, diseases and conditions, emergency health care, family planning, the human body, mental health, migrant health, nutrition and food sanitation, personal hygiene, physical fitness, prenatal and infant care, smoking and health.

*Arrangement:* Alphabetical by subjects listed above, then alphabetical by title.

*Entries:* Title or series title, type of medium, length, sound or silent, color or b/w, date, rental/purchase price, annotation, distributor code.

*Special Features:* Addendum (three filmstrips); list of distributors with addresses.

118. **Guide to Films on Asia.** Educational Resources/Asian Literature Program, The Asia Society, 112 E. Sixty-fourth St., New York, NY 10021. 1975. Free. 8p.

*Scope:* A highly selective list of 35 films on Asia based on evaluations done by area specialists and teachers during a December 1975 film festival. Films on Afghanistan, Bangladesh, China, India, Indonesia, Japan, Korea, Malaysia, Sri Lanka, Thailand, and Vietnam are included.

*Arrangement:* Alphabetical by country.

*Entries:* Distributor, color or b/w, purchase or rental price, year produced, length of film and a brief descriptive annotation.

*Special Features:* A list of 13 other sources of or guides to films on Asia.

119. **Guide to Free-Loan Films about Foreign Lands** (16mm). Serina Press, 70 Kennedy St., Alexandria, VA 22305. 1975. $12.95. 282p.

*Scope:* More than 3,000 films dealing with 76 foreign countries and from 97 sources. Some of the subject areas are: customs and culture, economics, politics, international relations, science, women, energy, pollution, music, dance, industry, painting, theater, sculpture, social concerns, sports, geography, agriculture, famous personalities, tourism, religion, folklore, medicine, ancient civilization, architecture, and wildlife. Most films have English sound. Countries include: Argentina, Australia, Austria, Barbados, Belgium, Bolivia, Botswana, Britain, Canada, Ceylon, Communist China, Republic of China, Colombia, Costa Rica, Czechoslovakia, Denmark, Ecuador, Egypt, Finland, France, Germany, Ghana, Greece, Guyana, Iceland, India, Indonesia, Iran, Ireland, Israel, Italy, Ivory Coast, Jamaica, Japan, Kenya, Korea, Kuwait, Lebanon, Lesotho, Libya, Liechtenstein, Luxembourg, Malaysia, Malawi, Mexico, Mongolia, Morocco, Nepal, Netherlands, New Zealand, Norway, Pakistan, Panama, Peru, Philippines, Poland, Portugal, Rhodesia, Saudi Arabia, Sikkim, Singapore, South Africa, Soviet Union, Spain, Sudan, Sweden, Switzerland, Thailand, Trinidad and Tobago, Tunisia, Turkey, Uganda, Venezuela, Vietnam, Yugoslavia, and Zambia.

*Arrangement:* Alphabetical by name of country and then alphabetical by title.

*Entries:* Title, running time, color or b/w, descriptive annotation.

*Special Features:* Subject index; list of sources.

120. **Guide to Free-Loan Films on the Urban Condition** (16mm). Serina Press, 70 Kennedy St., Alexandria, VA 22305. 1976. $7.95. 77p.

*Scope:* A list of over 500 films available on a free loan basis from 88 sources for public, nonprofit showing. The films cover a broad range of curriculum-oriented and general interest subjects relating to the "urban condition," e.g., air, water and noise pollution, alcoholism, bomb threats, drug abuse, driver education, crime, law enforcement, police, delinquency and the courts, smoking, prisons, inner city problems, self-defense, corruption in government, future shock, suicide, poverty, minority groups, racial discrimination, consumer interest, energy crisis, energy conservation, environmental protection, urban planning and renewal, transportation, social problems and services, welfare.

*Arrangement:* Alphabetical by subject area and then alphabetical by title.

*Entries:* Title, source, length, date, descriptive annotation.

*Special Features:* Title index; source index.

121. **Guide to Free-Loan Sports Films (16mm).** 2d ed. Serina Press, 70 Kennedy St., Alexandria, VA 22305. 1976. $6.95. 68p.

*Scope:* A list of over 800 sports films available for public, nonprofit showing on a free loan basis from approximately 80 sources. Films deal with all aspects of participation and spectator sports. Included are instructional and educational films, films on sports safety, films for entertainment, and films on training and officiating. Among the over 40 sports in the *Guide* are: archery, bowling, equestrianism, fishing, football, golf, gymnastics, hockey, hunting, ice skating, judo, la crosse, marksmanship, motorcycling, mountaineering, olympic competition, sailing, scuba diving, skiing, snowmobiling, soccer, softball, swimming, tennis, waterskiing, and many more.

*Arrangement:* Alphabetical by subject, and then alphabetical by title.

*Entries:* Title, source, length, date, descriptive annotation.

*Special Features:* Title index; source index.

122. **Guide to Free-Loan Training Films (16mm).** 2d ed. Serina Press, 70 Kennedy St., Alexandria, VA 22305. 1975. $7.95. 113p.

*Scope:* Approximately 900 films available for public, nonprofit exhibition on a free loan basis from over 150 sources. Subject areas include: automotive, bearings, construction, data processing, electricity, fire control, foundries, grinding, hydraulics, lubricants, machine tools, material handling, metals, motivation, office practices, photography, printing, retailing, steel, supervision, welding, woodworking, work methods, and many more.

*Arrangement:* Alphabetical by subject areas and then alphabetical by title.

*Entries:* Title, source, running time, color or b/w, descriptive annotation.

*Special Features:* Title index; list of sources.

123. **Guide to Government-Loan Films** (16mm)—Volume One, The Civilian Agencies. 4th ed. Serina Press, 70 Kennedy St., Alexandria, VA 22305. 1976. $9.95. 195p.

> *Scope:* More than 980 films and 88 filmstrips and slides of general and professional interest available from 63 federal government agencies on a free loan basis. Subjects include: career guidance, civics, history, government, consumerisn., home economics, sciences, environment, vocational education, art, social welfare, and health.
>
> *Arrangement:* Alphabetical by government agency and then alphabetical by title; some agency lists are arranged by subjects, then are alphabetical by title.
>
> *Entries:* Title, date, running time or number of slides, color or b/w, sound or silent, descriptive annotation, suggested audience.
>
> *Special Features:* Subject index; list of sources; index of agencies.

124. **Guide to Government-Loan Films** (16mm)—Volume Two, The Defense Agencies. 2d ed. Serina Press, 70 Kennedy St., Alexandria, VA 22305. 1976. $9.95. 176p.

> *Scope:* More than 1,770 motion pictures available on loan for public, nonprofit exhibiton, free of charge from the U.S. Army, U.S. Air Force, U.S. Navy, U.S. Marine Corps. Films cover a wide range of subjects of interest to students, faculty members, and the general public.
>
> *Arrangement:* By military branch, then by series number or alphabetical by title.
>
> *Entries:* Series number, title, date if available, running time, color or b/w, descriptive annotation.
>
> *Special Features:* Subject index; list of sources.

125. **Harrison Tape Guide.** Bimonthly. Weiss Publishing Corp., 143 W. Twentieth St., New York, NY 10011. Available at record and music stores, or from the publisher. $1 single issue; $5.50 yearly subscription.

> *Scope:* A list of over 30,000 prerecorded tapes in all configurations. Approximately one-fifth of the entries are classical music; the other categories are popular, country, jazz, shows and films, religious, Hawaiian, international, spoken, and children's.
>
> *Arrangement:* The catalog is divided into sections by type of tape format. Each section is subdivided into content categories. Popular, country and jazz tapes are listed alphabetically by last name

of performer; shows and films, by title except for miscellaneous collections; classical works, by composer; classical collections are arranged primarily by instrumentation (trumpet, guitar, orchestra), or by musical category or performers (concertos, Boston Pops, Ormandy, etc.). The remaining categories are alphabetical by performer, title, and/or author for spoken and children's tapes.

*Entries:* Composer (for classical entries), title, artist(s)/performing group, conductor, tape format, abbreviations for label and distributor, number, price.

126. **Health Careers Film Guide.** Bureau of Health Manpower Education, National Institutes of Health, U.S. Department of Health, Education, and Welfare, Bethesda, MD 20014. Available from the Superintendent of Documents, U.S. Government Printing Office, Washington, DC 20402. 1972. 35¢. 31p. (DHEW–PUB–NIH–72–306). Available also in microfiche and hard copy from ERIC Document Reproduction Service, P.O. Box 190, Arlington, VA 22210. Apply for current prices. ED 080 487.

*Scope:* This list represents a survey of the 16mm sound films available in 1972 concerning the field of health careers. The introduction indicates that a major criterion for selection was recency, although some older films that give a fairly accurate image of a profession were included, with some emphasis given to films useful for minority recruiting. The professions included are: audiology, speech pathology and education of the deaf, dentistry, dietetics, environmental health, general, hospital careers, medical records, medical technology, medicine, mental health, nursing, optometry and ophthalmology, pharmacy, public health, radiology and x-ray technology, rehabilitation, research, social work, veterinary science. The films are evaluated and appropriate audiences are suggested.

*Arrangement:* Alphabetical by the professions mentioned above.

*Entries:* Title, running time, color or b/w, date, free loan/rental/ purchase prices, description of content and evaluation, audience, distributor code.

*Special Features:* Directory of distributors.

127. **Helping Children Cope with Death and Separation: Resources for Teachers,** by Joanne Bernstein. Educational Resources Information Center/Early Childhood Education. Available from Publications Office/ICBD, College of Education, University of Illinois, 805 W. Pennsylvania Ave., Urbana, IL 61801. 1976. $1.85. 30p. (Catalog no.186)

*Scope:* Included in this compilation are selected and briefly anno-tated lists of children's books, films, filmstrips, and cassettes which treat death and separation. Also included are lists of materials for adults and a section of books and chapters in books about biblio-therapy. "Prior to publication the manuscript was submitted to the Area Committee for Early Childhood Education at the Uni-versity of Illniois for critical review and determination of profes-sional competence. This publication has met such standards. Points of view or opinions, however, do not necessarily represent the official view or opinions of either the Area Committee or the National Institute of Education" (Verso of title page).

*Arrangement:* By types of media and broad subjects mentioned above.

*Entries:* Author (print), publisher/producer/distributor, length in minutes/frames/number of items, color or b/w, date if available, grade level, purchase and/or rental price.

*Special Features:* Addresses of Media Distribution Centers; refer-ences (and abstracts) from *Research in Education;* references from *Current Index to Journals in Education;* "How to Order ERIC Documents"; ERIC Clearinghouse—Current Addresses.

128. **Hospital/Health Care Training Media Profiles.** Olympic Media In-formation, 71 W. Twenty-third St., New York, NY 10010. Bimonthly. 1974 to date. Apply for prices. 8½″ x 11″ loose-leaf format with one entry per page. (Cumulative index and sample pages free on letter-head request)

*Scope:* A comprehensive service which identifies, describes, and eval-uates films, filmstrips, media kits, and other types of audiovisual programs available from commercial and noncommercial sources. Subject categories include: nursing education, inservice education, continuing education, personnel training, administrative skills, team training, patient education, rehabilitation, laboratory skills, patient care, contemporary medical problems, the family, social and human values, community health. Each profile includes a detailed synopsis written by an audiovisual specialist, a factual description of the item, the intended audience, and an objective evaluation. At the close of each volume there is a cumulative title and subject index to all volumes.

*Arrangement:* By subject categories.

*Entries:* Title, subject area, length, type of medium, color or b/w, date, primary audience, content and treatment, components (kits), synopsis, discussion questions, related materials, evaluation, name and address of distributor who rents/loans/sells the item.

*Special Features:* Loose-leaf format with binders; volumes are completely revised two years after initial publication.

129. **Index to Bibliographies and Resource Materials: Project Media, Summer 1975.** National Indian Education Association, 3036 University Ave., S.E., Suite 3, Minneapolis, MN 55414. Available in microfiche and hard copy from ERIC Document Reproduction Service, P.O. Box 190, Arlington, VA 22210. 1975. Apply for current prices. 225p. ED 118 341.

*Scope:* A descriptive, annotated list of print and nonprint media by, for, or about native Americans. The work "represents some of the resource materials to be included in the functioning computer-housed data base now being constructed by Project Media" (Introduction). As a precursor of a printed catalog to be published as more data are gathered, the index includes the following types of entries: bibliographies (84 citations representative of 14,000 available bookforms, filmforms, audioforms, microforms, and realia), commercially produced resource materials, commercial film catalogs, periodicals, native American periodic publications, native American radio programming, native American tape services, radio stations interested in beginning native American programming, films, filmstrips, filmloops, records, cassettes, and reel-to-reel tapes.

*Arrangement:* By format categories, then alphabetical by author or title.

*Entries:* Author (print) title, format (nonbooks) date, color or b/w, sound or silent, length in pages/minutes/frames, circulation and editor (serials), price, publisher/producer/distributor, technical quality (nonprint), annotation.

*Special Features:* Title index to films, filmstrips, and filmloops; title index to records, cassettes, and reel-to-reel tapes.

130. **Index to Black History and Studies—Multimedia.** 2d ed. National Information Center for Educational Media, University of Southern California, University Park, Los Angeles, CA 90007. 1973. $19.50 postpaid in the U.S. and Canada. 176p.

*Scope:* Approximately 10,000 titles of 16mm educational motion pictures, filmstrips, 8mm motion cartridges, videotapes, audiotapes, overhead transparencies, records, and slides are indexed and described in this revised edition. Like its predecessors, the *Index* was compiled from information stored in the NICEM data bank and includes the following subjects: Africa—culture, Africa past, Afro-America, arts and crafts, agriculture, business, civil rights, economic conditions, education, employment, famous personalities, history, housing, literature, other countries, professions, recreation and sports, religions, segregation and integration, social problems, songs and music, Civil War period. The films range from preschool through elementary, secondary, college, university, adult and professional audience levels.

*Arrangement:* Main section, the "Alphabetical Guide to Black History and Studies—Multimedia," includes individual titles and series titles, arranged by computer alphabetizing; the section entitled "Subject Guide to Black History and Studies—Multimedia" arranges titles alphabetically under the subjects listed above.

*Entries:* Main section—title or series title, type of medium and description of format, color code, length in minutes/frames, audience or grade level code, description of content, individual titles if a series, producer and distributor codes, year of release, Library of Congress catalog card number when available.

*Special Features:* "How to Use This Index," "Subject Heading Outline," "Index to Subject Headings," "Directory of Producers and Distributors," part 1, arranged alphabetically by code and including addresses; part 2, arranged alphabetically by name.

131. **Index to Computer Based Learning,** edited by Robert E. Hoye and Anastasia C. Wang. 4th ed. Copyrighted by the Regents of the University of Wisconsin. Available from Educational Technology Publications, 140 Sylvan Ave., Englewood Cliffs, NJ 07632. 1973. $18.95. 704p. Former title: *Index to Computer Assisted Instruction.*

*Scope:* A listing of 1,766 computer based instructional programs in school subjects ranging from primary to college and adult education. Designed as an availability source guide for persons interested in computer based learning research and development and faculty members interested in using computer based learning to augment their instructional techniques. Information provided with each program listing should make it possible for cooperation to develop among program developers. Includes 98 subject matter areas: accounting, aeronautics, agriculture, airline reservations, anthropology, Arabic, art, astronomy, banking, behavioral science, biochemistry, biology, botany, Bulgarian, business, chemistry, Chinese, climatology, commerce, communications, CAI laboratory management, computer operations and programming, computer systems and utility programs, demography, demonstrations and games, driver education, Dutch, economics, education, educational and instructional research, electricity, electronics, engineering, English, Esperanto, fingerspelling, fishery, food science, foreign languages, French, genetics, geography, geology, German, graphic arts, guidance and counseling, health professions, history of Canada, history of the United Sates, history of Western civilization, home economics, humanities, industrial arts, information retrieval, intelligence testing, Italian, Japanese, journalism, language arts, Latin, law, law enforcement, library science, literature, logic, management, mathematics, mechanics, military training, music, natural resources, personnel, philosophy, physics, physiology, political science, printing, programmed instruction, psychology, reading, religion, Russian, science, Slavic, social sciences, social welfare, sociology, Spanish, speech pathology and audiology, spelling, statistics, student opinion survey, student response analysis, system planning, visual perception, vocational rehabilitation, weapon system acquisition process, zoology.

*Arrangement:* Alphabetical by subject and then by title.

*Entries:* Title, author, source, description, prerequisites, level of instruction, type of student, total hours of instruction available, average student completion time, instructional strategy, instructional logic, use of program, supplementary equipment/materials, status of program, availability of program, funding/sponsoring agency, descriptive literature, language of the program, central processor, terminal description, applications.

*Special Features:* Listing by central processor; listing by programming language; listing by instructional strategy; listing by source; new organizations and related activities; program questionnaire.

132. **Index to Educational Audio Tapes.** 4th ed. National Information Center for Educational Media, University of Southern California, University Park, Los Angeles, CA 90007. 1976. Revised biennially and supplemented in alternate years by *NICEM Update of Nonbook Media* (for details see entry no.180). $47 postpaid in the U.S. and Canada; $23.50 microfiche; discounts for biennial subscription to all NICEM *Indexes.*

*Scope:* Approximately 28,000 titles of educational audiotapes are indexed and described in this expanded edition. Like its predecessors, the *Index* was compiled from information stored in the NICEM data bank and includes audiotapes on the following subjects: agriculture, biography, business and economics, civics and political systems, education, English language, fine arts, foreign language, geography, guidance, health and safety, history, home economics, industrial and technical education, literature, mathematics, physical education and recreation, psychology, religion and philosophy, natural and physical sciences, social science, sociology. The tapes range from preschool through elementary, secondary, college, university, adult, professional, industrial, religious, teacher, and special audience levels.

*Arrangement:* Main section, the "Alphabetical Guide to Educational Audio Tapes," includes individual titles and series titles, arranged by computer alphabetizing; the section entitled "Subject Guide to Educational Audio Tapes" lists titles alphabetically under 26 broad headings and numerous subheadings.

*Entries:* Main section—title or series title, size and physical description, length, monaural/stereo or both, audience or grade level code, description of content, individual titles if a series, producer and distributor codes.

*Special Features:* "How to Use This Index," "Subject Heading Outline," "Index to Subject Headings," "Directory of Producers and Distributors," part 1, arranged alphabetically by code and including addresses; part 2, arranged alphabetically by name.

133. **Index to Educational Overhead Transparencies.** 5th ed. National Information Center for Educational Media, University of Southern California, University Park, Los Angeles, CA 90007. 1976. Revised biennially and supplemented in alternate years by *NICEM Update of Nonbook Media* (for details see entry no.180). $75.50 postpaid in the U.S. and Canada; $39.50 microfiche; discounts for biennial subscription to all NICEM *Indexes.* 2v.

*Scope:* Approximately 60,000 titles of commercially produced transparencies are indexed and described in this revised and enlarged edition. Like its predecessors, the *Index* was compiled from information stored in the NICEM data bank and includes the following subjects: agriculture, biography, business and economics, civics and political systems, education, English language, fine arts, foreign language, geography, guidance, health and safety, history, home economics, industrial and technical education, literature, mathematics, physical education and recreation, psychology, religion and philosophy, natural and physical sciences, social science, sociology. The transparencies range from preschool through elementary, secondary, college, university, and adult audience levels.

*Arrangement:* Main section, the "Alphabetical Guide to Educational Overhead Transparencies," includes individual titles and series titles, arranged by computer alphabetizing and divided between the two volumes; the section entitled "Subject Guide to Educational Overhead Transparencies" appears in the first volume and lists titles alphabetically under 26 broad headings and numerous subheadings.

*Entries:* Main section—title or series title, size and physical description, number of overlays, stock or color code, audience or grade level code, description of content, individual titles if a series, producer and distributor codes, year of release.

*Special Features:* "How to Use This Index," "Subject Heading Outline," "Index to Subject Headings," "Directory of Producers and Distributors," part 1, arranged alphabetically by code and including addresses; part 2, arranged alphabetically by name.

**134. Index to Educational Records.** 4th ed. National Information Center for Educational Media, University of Southern California, University Park, Los Angeles, CA 90007. 1976. Revised biennially and supplemented in alternate years by *NICEM Update of Nonbook Media* (for details see entry no.180). $47 postpaid in the U.S. and Canada; $23.50 microfiche; discounts for biennial subscription to all NICEM *Indexes.* 746p.

*Scope:* Approximately 25,000 titles of musical and nonmusical phonodiscs are indexed and described in this edition. Like its predecessors, the *Index* was compiled from information stored in the NICEM data bank and includes discs on the following subjects: agriculture, biography, business and economics, civics and political systems, education, English language, fine arts, foreign language, geography, guidance, health and safety, history, home economics, industrial and technical education, literature, mathematics, physical education and recreation, psychology, religion and philosophy, the natural and physical sciences, social science, and sociology. The titles range from the preschool level through elementary, secondary, college, and adult audience levels.

*Arrangement:* Main section, the "Alphabetical Guide to Educational Records," includes individual titles and series titles, arranged by computer alphabetizing; the section entitled "Subject Guide to Educational Records" lists titles alphabetically under 26 broad headings and numerous subheadings.

*Entries:* Main section—title, composer/author, size and speed, number of sides, monaural/stereo or both, audience or grade level code, description of content, individual titles of a series or album, producer and distributor codes, year of release, Library of Congress catalog card number when available.

*Special Features:* "How to Use This Index," "Subject Heading Outline," "Index to Subject Headings," "Directory of Producers and Distributors," part 1, arranged alphabetically by code and including addresses; part 2, arranged alphabetically by name.

135. **Index to Educational Slides.** 3d ed. National Information Center for Educational Media, University of Southern California, University Park, Los Angeles, CA 90007. 1976. Revised biennially and supplemented in alternate years by *NICEM Update of Nonbook Media* (for details see entry no.180). $42.50 postpaid in the U.S. and Canada; $22 microfiche; discounts for biennial subscription to all NICEM *Indexes.*

*Scope:* Approximately 28,000 titles of educational slides are indexed in this revised edition. Like its predecessors, the *Index* was compiled from information stored in the NICEM data bank and includes slides on the following subjects: agriculture, biography, business and economics, civics and political systems, education, English language, fine arts, foreign language, geography, guidance, health and safety, history, home economics, industrial and technical education, literature, mathematics, physical education, psychology, religion and philosophy, natural and physical sciences, social sciences, sociology. The slides range from preschool through elementary, secondary, college, university, and adult audience levels.

*Arrangement:* Main section, the "Alphabetical Guide to Educational Slides," includes individual titles and series titles arranged by computer alphabetizing; the section entitled "Subject Guide to Educational Slides" lists titles alphabetically under 26 broad headings and numerous subheadings.

*Entries:* Main section—title or series title, size and physical description, stock or color code, number of slides in set, description of content for some entries, producer/distributor codes, year of release if available.

*Special Features:* "How to Use This Index," "Subject Heading Outline," "Index to Subject Headings," "Directory of Producers and Distributors," part 1, arranged alphabetically by code and including addresses; part 2, arranged alphabetically by name.

136. **Index to Educational Video Tapes.** 4th ed. National Information Center for Educational Media, University of Southern California, University Park, Los Angeles, CA 90007. 1976. Revised biennially and supplemented in alternate years by *NICEM Update of Nonbook Media* (for details see entry no.180). $29.50 postpaid in the U.S. and Canada; $14.50 microfiche; discounts for biennial subscription to all NICEM *Indexes.* 410p.

*Scope:* Approximately 15,000 titles of educational videotapes are indexed and described in this revised edition. Like its predecessors, the *Index* was compiled from information stored in the

NICEM data bank and includes videotapes on the following subjects: agriculture, biography, business and economics, civics and political systems, education, English language, fine arts, foreign language, geography, guidance, health and safety, history, home economics, industrial and technical education, literature, mathematics, physical education and recreation, psychology, religion and philosophy, natural and physical sciences, social science, sociology. The videotapes range from preschool through elementary, secondary, college, university and adult audience levels.

*Arrangement:* Main section, the "Alphabetical Guide," includes individual titles and series titles, arranged by computer alphabetizing; the section entitled "Subject Guide to Educational Video Tapes" lists titles alphabetically under 26 broad headings and numerous subheadings.

*Entries:* Main section—title or series title, size and physical description, length, stock or color code, audience or grade level code, description of content, individual titles if a series, producer and distributor codes, production credit codes, year of release, broadcast quality.

*Special Features:* "How to Use This Index," "Subject Heading Outline," "Index to Subject Headings," "Directory of Producers and Distributors," part 1, arranged alphabetically by code and including addresses; part 2, arranged alphabetically by name.

137. **Index to 8mm Motion Cartridges.** 5th ed. National Information Center for Educational Media, University of Southern California, University Park, Los Angeles, CA 90007. 1976. Revised biennially and supplemented in alternate years by *NICEM Update of Nonbook Media* (for details see entry no.180). $47 postpaid in the U.S. and Canada; $23.50 microfiche; discounts for biennial subscription to all NICEM *Indexes.* 589p.

*Scope:* Approximately 26,000 titles of commercially produced standard-8mm and super-8mm sound and silent motion cartridges are indexed and described in this expanded edition. Like its predecessors, the *Index* was compiled from information stored in the NICEM data bank and includes 8mm motion cartridges on the following subjects: agriculture, biography, business and economics, civics and political systems, education, English language, fine arts, foreign language, geography, guidance, health and safety, history, home economics, industrial and technical education, literature, mathematics, physical education and recreation, psychology, religion and philosophy, natural and physical sciences, social science, sociology. The titles range from preschool through elementary, secondary, college, and adult audience levels.

*Arrangement:* Main section, the "Alphabetical Guide to 8mm Motion Cartridges," includes individual titles and series titles, arranged by computer alphabetizing; the section entitled "Subject Guide to 8mm Motion Cartridges" lists titles alphabetically under 26 broad headings and numerous subheadings.

*Entries:* Main section—title or series title, size and physical description, length, stock or color code, audience or grade level code, description of content, individual titles if a series, producer and distributor codes, year of release, Library of Congress catalog card number when available.

*Special Features:* "How to Use This Index," "Subject Heading Outline," "Index to Subject Headings," "Directory of Producers and Distributors," part 1, arranged alphabetically by code and including addresses; part 2, arranged alphabetically by name.

138. **Index to Environmental Studies—Multimedia.** National Information Center for Educational Media, University of Southern California, University Park, Los Angeles, CA 90007. 1976. Revised biennially and supplemented in alternate years by *NICEM Update of Nonbook Media* (for details see entry no.180). $34.50 postpaid in the U.S. and Canada; $18.50 microfiche; discounts for biennial subscription to all NICEM *Indexes.* 1,113p.

*Scope:* Approximately 26,000 titles of educational films, filmstrips, 8mm motion cartridges, audiotapes, records, videotapes, overhead transparencies, and slides are described and indexed in this revised edition. Like those in the companion NICEM indexes, these titles are those stored in the computerized data bank and include the following broad subjects: amphibians, bioclimatology, botany, birth control, balance of nature, city planning, desert animals, desert plants, evaluation, fresh water ecology, food chains, farming, geographical distribution, genetics, mountains, polar regions, oceanography, reproduction, soil management, and sea life. The materials range from elementary, junior and senior high school through college, university, adult, and professional audience levels.

*Arrangement:* Main section, the "Alphabetical Guide to Environmental Studies—Multimedia," is alphabetical by title or series title; the "Subject Guide to Environmental Studies—Multimedia" lists titles alphabetically under broad subject headings and numerous subheadings.

*Entries:* Main section—title or series title, type of medium and description of format, color code, length in minutes/frames, grade level code, brief content description, individual titles if a series,

Library of Congress catalog card number, producer and distributor codes, date.

*Special Features:* "How to Use This Index," "Subject Heading Outline," "Index to Subject Headings," "Directory of Producers and Distributors," part 1, arranged alphabetically by code and including addresses; part 2, arranged alphabetically by name.

139. **Index to Health and Safety Education—Multimedia.** 3d ed. National Information Center for Educational Media, University of Southern California, University Park, Los Angeles, CA 90007. 1976. Revised biennially and supplemented in alternate years by *NICEM Update of Nonbook Media* (for details see entry no.180). $47 postpaid in the U.S. and Canada; $23.50 microfiche; discounts for biennial subscription to all NICEM *Indexes.* 1,141p.

*Scope:* Approximately 33,000 titles of educational films, filmstrips, 8mm motion cartridges, videotapes, records, audiotapes, overhead transparencies, and slides are included in this revised edition. Like those in the companion NICEM indexes, these titles are those stored in the computerized data bank and include the following health and safety subjects: alcohol, dental care, diet, sanitation, home and community safety, playground and school safety, sexual hygiene, sleep, smoking, venereal disease, ventilation, water fluoridation, home economics, home management, nursing, physical education, athletics, coaching, sports, basic life science, biology, and many more.

*Arrangement:* Main section, the "Alphabetical Guide to Health and Safety Education—Multimedia," is alphabetical by title or series title; the "Subject Guide to Health and Safety Education—Multimedia" lists titles alphabetically under numerous subject headings.

*Entries:* Main section—title or series title, type of medium and description of format, color code, length in minutes/frames, grade level code, brief content description, individual titles if a series, Library of Congress catalog card number when available, producer and distributor codes, date.

*Special Features:* "How to Use This Index," "Subject Heading Outline," "Index to Subject Headings," "Directory of Producers and Distributors," part 1, arranged alphabetically by code and including addresses; part 2, arranged alphabetically by name.

140. **Index to Psychology—Multimedia.** 3d ed. National Information Center for Educational Media, University of Southern California, University Park, Los Angeles, CA 90007. 1976. Revised biennially and supplemented in alternate years by *NICEM Update of Nonbook*

*Media* (for details see entry no.180). $47 postpaid in the U.S. and Canada; $23.50 microfiche; discounts for biennial subscription to all NICEM *Indexes.* 1,021p.

*Scope:* Approximately 28,000 titles of educational films, filmstrips, 8mm motion cartridges, videotapes, records, audiotapes, overhead transparencies, and slides are included in this revised edition. Like those in the companion NICEM indexes, these titles are those stored in the computerized data bank and include the following broad fields: psychology (general), animal, clinical, developmental, educational, experimental, methodology and research technology, personality, physiological, and social.

*Arrangement:* Main section, the "Alphabetical Guide to Psychology—Multimedia," is alphabetical by title or series title; the "Subject Guide to Psychology—Multimedia" lists titles alphabetically under broad subjects and numerous subheadings.

*Entries:* Main section—title or series title, type of medium and description of format, color code, length in minutes/frames, audience or grade level code, brief description, individual titles if a series, Library of Congress catalog card number when available, producer and distributor codes, date.

*Special Features:* "How to Use This Index," "Subject Heading Outline," "Index to Subject Headings," "Directory of Producers and Distributors," part 1, arranged alphabetically by code and including addresses; part 2, arranged alphabetically by name.

141. **Index to 16mm Educational Films.** 6th ed. National Information Center for Educational Media, University of Southern California, University Park, Los Angeles, CA 90007. 1976. Revised biennially and supplemented in alternate years by *NICEM Update of Nonbook Media* (for details see entry no.180). $109.50 postpaid in the U.S. and Canada; $67.50 microfiche; discounts for biennial subscription to all NICEM *Indexes.* 4v.

*Scope:* Approximately 100,000 titles of 16mm educational motion pictures (almost all with optical sound) are indexed and described in this greatly expanded edition. Like its predecessors, the *Index* was compiled from information stored in the NICEM data bank and includes films on the following subjects: agriculture, biography, business and economics, civics and political systems, education, English language, fine arts, foreign language, geography, guidance, health and safety, history, home economics, industrial and technical education, literature, mathematics, physical education and recreation, psychology, religion and philosophy, natural and physical sciences, social science, sociology. The films range from preschool through elementary, secondary, college, university, adult, professional (law, medicine, etc.), industrial, religious, teacher, and special audience levels.

*Arrangement:* Main section, the "Alphabetical Guide to 16mm Films," includes individual titles and series titles, arranged by computer alphabetizing and distributed among the last three volumes; the section entitled "Subject Guide to 16mm Films" appears in the first volume and lists titles alphabetically under 26 broad headings and 399 subheadings.

*Entries:* Main section—title or series title, edition or version, length, stock or color code, audience or grade level, description of content, individual titles if a series, producer and distributor codes, production credit codes, year of release, Library of Congress catalog card number when available.

*Special Features:* "How to Use This Index," "Subject Heading Outline," "Index to Subject Headings," "Directory of Producers and Distributors," part 1, arranged alphabetically by code and including addresses; part 2, arranged alphabetically by name. These features appear in the first volume.

**142. Index to 35mm Educational Filmstrips.** 6th ed. National Information Center for Educational Media, University of Southern California, University Park, Los Angeles, CA 90007. 1976. Revised biennially and supplemented in alternate years by *NICEM Update of Nonbook Media* (for details see entry no.180). $86.50 postpaid in the U.S. and Canada; $45.50 microfiche; discounts for biennial subscription to all NICEM *Indexes.* 3v.

*Scope:* Approximately 70,000 filmstrips with and without sound and captions are indexed and described in this greatly expanded edition. Like its predecessors, the *Index* was compiled from information stored in the NICEM data bank and includes filmstrips on the following subjects: agriculture, biography, business and economics, civics and political systems, education, English language, fine arts, foreign language, geography, guidance, health and safety, history, home economics, industrial and technical education, literature, mathematics, physical education and recreation, psychology, religion and philosophy, natural and physical sciences, social science, sociology. The filmstrips range from preschool through elementary, secondary, college, university, adult, professional (law, medicine, etc.), industrial, religious, teacher, and special audience levels.

*Arrangement:* Main section, the "Alphabetical Guide to 35mm Filmstrips," includes individual titles and series titles, arranged by computer alphabetizing and distributed among the volumes; the section entitled "Subject Guide to 35mm Filmstrips" appears in the first volume and lists titles alphabetically under 26 broad headings and numerous subheadings.

*Entries:* Main section—title or series title, size and physical description, number of frames, stock or color code, audience or grade level, description of content, individual titles if a series, producer and distributor codes, year of release, Library of Congress catalog card number when available.

*Special Features:* "How to Use This Index," "Subject Heading Outline," "Index to Subject Headings," "Directory of Producers and Distributors," part 1, arranged alphabetically by code and including addresses; part 2, arranged alphabetically by name.

143. **Index to Vocational and Technical Education—Multimedia.** 3d ed. National Information Center for Educational Media, University of Southern California, University Park, Los Angeles, CA 90007. 1976. Revised biennially and supplemented in alternate years by *NICEM Update of Nonbook Media* (for details see entry no.180). $47 postpaid in the U.S. and Canada; $23.50 microfiche; discounts for biennial subscription to all NICEM *Indexes.* 936p.

*Scope:* There are approximately 32,000 titles of educational films, filmstrips, 8mm motion cartridges, videotapes, records, audiotapes, overhead transparencies, and slides in this revised edition. Like those included in the companion NICEM indexes, these titles are those stored in the computerized data bank and include the following broad subjects: guidance and counseling, automation, automobile, aviation, construction, electrical work, electronics, engineering, engines and power systems, machine shop and metal work, mechanical and engineering drawing, photography, plastics, plumbing, printing and graphic arts, refrigeration, woodwork, and vocations. The materials range from intermediate and junior high through college, adult, and professional-industrial audience levels.

*Arrangement:* Main section, the "Alphabetical Guide to Vocational and Technical Education—Multimedia," is alphabetical by title or series title; the "Subject Guide to Vocational and Technical Education—Multimedia" lists titles alphabetically under broad subject headings and numerous subheadings.

*Entries:* Main section—title or series title, type of medium and description of format, color code, length in minutes/frames, grade level code, brief content description, individual titles if a series, Library of Congress catalog card number when available, producer and distributor codes, date.

*Special Features:* "How to Use This Index," "Subject Heading Outline," "Index to Subject Headings," "Directory of Producers and
Distributors," part 1, arranged alphabetically by code and including addresses; part 2, arranged alphabetically by name.

144. **Instructional Materials for Career Education.** Institute of Research
and Development in Occupational Education, Department of Education, New York State College of Agriculture and Life Sciences,
Cornell University, Ithaca, NY 14850, in cooperation with the Bureau
of Inservice Education, New York State Education Department,
Albany, NY 12224. Available in microfiche and hard copy from ERIC
Document Reproduction Service, P.O. Box 190, Arlington, VA 22210.
1975. Apply for current prices. 283p. ED 122 069. (See also related
document *Instructional Materials for Occupational Education.* ED
122 068)

*Scope:* This resource guide is the second phase of a project during
which 92 career education teachers in the state of New York
participated in the evaluation of instructional materials for kindergarten through grade 8. An assessment instrument was
developed and used in evaluating the materials which include:
textbooks, posters, workbooks, audiovisual kits, pamphlets, cassette tapes, teachers' manuals, slides, transparencies, reference
books, and multimedia programs. Materials are grouped by grade
levels: kindergarten to 1, 2 to 3, 4 to 6, and 7 to 8. The assessment
includes a description of the material, the readability level for
printed material (Dale-Chall, Fry, or Spache formula), an overall
rating expressed as a ratio of total points (excellent, useful, unacceptable), and a summary of ratings (bias, accuracy, appropriateness, verbal and visual fluency, usefulness and versatility).
*Arrangement:* By subject area and/or grade level.
*Entries:* Subject area, title, author when known, publisher, date,
type of material and number of items, brief description of content,
readability grade level, overall rating, summary of ratings, additional comments.
*Special Features:* Assessment instrument.

145. **Instructional Materials for Occupational Education.** Institute of Re-
search and Development in Occupational Education, Department of
Education, New York State College of Agriculture and Life Sciences,
Cornell University, Ithaca, NY 14850, in cooperation with the Bureau
of Inservice Education, New York State Education Department,
Albany, NY 12224. Available in microfiche and hard copy from ERIC
Document Reproduction Service, P.O. Box 190, Arlington, VA 22210.

1975. Apply for current prices. 545p. ED 122 068. (See also related document *Instructional Materials for Career Education*. ED 122 069)

*Scope:* A task force of 84 occupational education high school teachers in the state of New York, selected and trained in the assessment process, developed this comprehensive list of manuals, workbooks, pamphlets, reference books, textbooks, periodicals, pictures, posters, audiotapes, transparencies, filmstrips, slide sets, records, and manipulation devices such as puzzles, games, puppets, and laboratory kits. The materials are grouped into sections by subject: automobile mechanics, building trades, business and office education, cosmetology, distributive education, and practical nursing. An assessment instrument, developed and used in the evaluation process, includes not only a description of the material but also the readability level for printed information (Dale-Chall, Frye, or Spache formula), an overall rating expressed as a ratio of total points (excellent, useful, unacceptable), and a summary of ratings (bias, accuracy, appropriateness, verbal and visual fluency, usefulness and versatility).

*Arrangement:* By subject areas in the order mentioned above.

*Entries:* Subject area, title, author when known, publisher, date, type of material and number of items, brief description of content, readability grade level, overall rating, summary of ratings, additional comments.

*Special Features:* Assessment instrument.

146. **Instructional Materials for Science,** by Dick Shea. California Learning Resource Center, 600 S. Commonwealth Ave., Suite 1304, Los Angeles, CA 90005. Available in microfiche and hard copy from ERIC Document Reproduction Service, P.O. Box 190, Arlington, VA 22210. 1974. Apply for current prices. 50p. ED 091 892.

*Scope:* A selected annotated list of approximately 270 films, filmstrips, filmloops, overhead transparencies, cassettes, records, instructional tapes, programmed materials, and texts for use with handicapped or normal children from kindergarten through grade 12. The materials are concerned with physical science, earth science, ecology, life science, general science, scientific method, and experimental science.

*Arrangement:* Alphabetical by publisher/producer.

*Entries:* Code for publisher/producer with name and address, title, order number, price, brief description, content area, grade level, asterisk denoting material developed for special education.

*Special Features:* Table of abbreviations used throughout the bibliography; index to materials by grade levels.

147. **Instructional Materials for Teaching the Use of the Library,** by Shirley L. Hopkinson. 5th ed. Claremont House, 231 E. San Fernando St., San Jose, CA 95112. 1975. $2.50 plus 25¢ postage. 94p.

*Scope:* An annotated, selected list of films, filmstrips, audiotapes, charts, books, tests, transparencies, and other aids, most of which have been produced since 1960 and designed to aid in teaching library use at the elementary school, high school, and college level. There are 75 motion pictures and 111 titles of individual filmstrips or series of filmstrips in this expanded edition.

*Arrangement:* By type of medium in six categories, then alphabetical by title or author.

*Entries:* Title, author, producer/publisher, date, length in minutes/ frames/pages/items, color or b/w, price, source, series, guide or manual, grade level, annotation summarizing content.

*Special Features:* Directory of producers, publishers, and other sources.

148. **International Index to Multi-Media Information,** edited by Wesley A. Doak and William J. Speed. 1970 to date. Quarterly. Audio-Visual Associates, 180 E. California Blvd., Pasadena, CA 91105. 1973, 1974. $36 per year; 1975. $60. (Continues *Film Review Index*). (A three-year cumulation of volumes one, two, and three, the *International Index to Multi-Media Information 1970–1972,* is published by Audio-Visual Associates and distributed by R. R. Bowker Company, 1180 Avenue of the Americas, New York, NY 10036. 1975. $30. 465p.)

*Scope:* A selective index to media reviews appearing in more than 110 periodicals. Included are 16mm films, filmloops, feature films, filmstrips, audiocassettes, discs, slides, transparencies, and multi-media kits. Brief excerpts from the reviews are quoted. Audience levels range from prekindergarten through college and adult.

*Arrangement:* Alphabetical by title.

*Entries:* Title, series title, producer, date, distributor or label and number, type of medium, sound or silent, color or b/w, length, sales price(s), Library of Congress catalog card number if available, suggested classification numbers, citation to review (periodical, volume, number, month, pages, reviewer, brief quotation), audience level, subject/author headings, series title cross references.

*Special Features:* Subject index; producer/distributor section.

149. **K-14 Career Education Multi-Media Catalogue.** Lakeshore Technical Institute, Sheboygan Public Schools, 830 Virginia Ave., Sheboygan, WI 53081. Available in microfiche and hard copy from ERIC

Document Reproduction Service, P.O. Box 190, Arlington, VA 22210. [1972]. Apply for current prices. 129p. ED 075 639.

*Scope:* "All of the materials in this catalog have been used. Most of them have been found to be valuable. However, some of these materials are not recommended" (Table of Contents). The list includes filmstrips, records, cassettes, microfiche, transparencies, 16mm films, books, magazines, slides, videotapes, self-instructional devices, and prints concerned with career attitudes, career orientation, career exploration, career preparation, vocational and adult education.

*Arrangement:* By grade level, then by type of medium and code number.

*Entries:* Code number, title or series title, producer/distributor/publisher, description of content, accompanying material if any, individual titles if a series.

*Special Features:* List of equipment.

150. **Landers Film Reviews,** published by Landers Associates, P.O. Box 69760, Los Angeles, CA 90069. June 1956 to date. $35 per year. Bi-monthly. (starting with v.20—five times a year, September through May)

*Scope:* Comprehensive reviews of 170 to 200 current 16mm films each issue in all subjects, including instructional, documentary, avant-garde, television documentary, industrial message film, American and foreign short subjects, children's fiction films and other general interest, nontheatrical films, covering releases of approximately 1,000 producers with new producers added frequently. Reports on award-winning films in American and foreign film festivals. Listing of new multimedia materials: filmstrips, disc and tape recordings, still photographs, overhead transparencies, posters, added in volume 15 (1970) as a continuing service.

*Arrangement:* 8½" x 11" loose-leaf sheets used through volume 18, changed to bound issue with volume 19. Film reviews arranged in alphabetical order in each issue, numerical paging by the volume (September through May). Subject and title indexes in each issue, cumulated indexes by the volume.

*Entries:* Title, distributor, producer, date of release, running time, color or b/w, cost for purchase or rental, interest level, descriptive and evaluative review in 150–250 words.

*Special Features:* Loose-leaf binder furnished for back volumes through volume 18. Library slip-case furnished for volume 19 and to date. Source directory with up-to-date addresses of producers and distributors included in each issue.

151. **Latin America: Sights and Sounds, A Guide to Motion Pictures and Music for College Courses,** by Jane M. Loy. Consortium of Latin American Studies Programs, Box 13362, University Station, Gainesville, FL 32604. 1973. $2.50; $1.50 to members of the Consortium and of the Latin American Studies Association. 243p. (CLASP Publication no.5)

*Scope:* A highly selected guide to 16mm and feature films suitable for college courses which deal with Latin America. Among the large number of 16mm films evaluated, 64 were judged acceptable and 66 were not recommended. The 13 feature films included are those which were reviewed favorably or which have been used successfully at the University of Massachusetts, Amherst. The recommended titles are concerned with the individual countries of Latin America and with the following topics: agrarian reform, anthropology, archaeology, architecture, art, biography, geography, government, history, Indians, literature, music, Negroes, population, religion, theater, and United States foreign relations.

*Arrangement:* The main body lists recommended 16mm films in two sections—an alphabetical subject heading index with titles included alphabetically under subjects, and an alphabetical title description index. The list of films previewed but not recommended and the list of feature films are arranged alphabetically by title; the "not recommended" list is preceded by a discussion of the seven weaknesses which are common in educational films about Latin America and includes titles which embody one or more of these weaknesses.

*Entries:* "Title Description Index" for 16mm films: title, country, color or b/w, length, producer, date of release, distributor and rental fee, synopsis of factual and photographic data, detailed critique of the film in one or more paragraphs, overall evaluation (excellent, good, average), suggested readings, audience and courses for which the film might be suited. Entries for feature films: title, country, color or b/w, length, language, producer, date of release, director, actors, distributor, price, synopsis, review sources, appraisal, suggested readings, overall evaluation (excellent, good, average, fair, poor).

*Special Features:* Introduction which describes the project to prepare the guide, the methodology used, and information on the value of films for college classrooms; a section explaining the use of the guide; list of distributors; a bibliography of film-related materials; an article on the teaching of Latin American music by Robert Stevenson, University of California, Los Angeles.

**152. Let's See It Again: Free Films for Elementary Schools,** by J. A. Kislia. Cebco Standard Publishing, Cebco Pflaum, 9 Kulick Rd., Fairfield, NJ 07006. 1975. $2.95. 126p.

*Scope:* A list of 212 critically annotated and rated 16mm films culled from the collections of six different kinds of agencies which lend films freely. More than 400 films were viewed by the author, by elementary school teachers, and by children in the selection of the final choices. The titles are rated on a scale ranging from "poor" to "excellent"; several of the films are judged suitable for high school and adult audiences as well as elementary school pupils. Introductory sections of the book discuss children's and teachers' reactions to the films, the rating scale, how and where to obtain free films, and some of the pitfalls in the process.

*Arrangement:* Alphabetical by title.

*Entries:* Title, color or b/w, running time, rating, audience level, subject, producer/distributor codes, date, description and evaluation, teacher evaluation if any, children's evaluation if any, two asterisks if title is usable through high school level.

*Special Features:* Subject index; alphabetical list of film titles; sources index; codes for producers and distributors.

**153. Library of Congress Catalogs: Films and Other Materials for Projection.** Washington, DC. 1973–date. Issued in 3 quarterly publications (January-March, April-June, July-September) with annual and quinquennial cumulations. Available from the Cataloging Distribution Service Division, Library of Congress, Building No. 159, Navy Yard Annex, Washington, DC 20541. 1973, 1974. $40 each; 1975. $50; 1976. $60. Sent without cost to all subscribers to the *National Union Catalog.* (Continues the *Library of Congress Catalog: Motion Pictures and Flmstrips* issued as part of the *National Union Catalog:* 1953–57, 1958–62; 1963–67, 1968–72)

*Scope:* The catalog includes all motion pictures, filmstrips, sets of transparencies, slide sets, and videorecordings cataloged by the Library of Congress, released in the United States and Canada, and which are considered to have educational or instructional value. Cataloging data are supplied mainly by producers, manufacturers, film libraries, or distributing agencies.

*Arrangement:* Alphabetical by title or author.

*Entries:* Title, type of medium, author or producer, location of offices of releaser or distributor, releaser or distributor, date, length—running time, number of slides, frames, etc.—sound, color or b/w, credits, summary, subject headings, Library of Congress Classification number, Dewey Decimal Classification number, Library of Congress catalog card number, name of reporting organization or institution. Added entries are made for producers, titles, authors, and authors and titles of published work upon which the material is based.

*Special Features:* List of *Library of Congress Catalogs* in book form, with sources and prices; elements of entries; filing arrangement; annual issues contain directory of producers and distributors and a subject index; entries also available in card form.

154. **Library of Congress Catalogs: Music, Books on Music, and Sound Recordings.** Washington, DC. 1973 to date. Issued semiannually with annual and quinquennial cumulations. Available from the Cataloging Distribution Service Division, Library of Congress, Building No. 159, Navy Yard Annex, Washington, DC 20541. 1973, 1974. $30 each; 1975. $35; 1976. $45. Sent without charge to all subscribers to the *National Union Catalog.* (Continues the *Library of Congress Catalog: Music and Phonorecords* issued as part of the *National Union Catalog:* 1953–57, 1958–62, 1963–67, 1968–72)

*Scope:* Music scores, sheet music, libretti, and books about music and musicians, sound recordings of all kinds—whether musical, educational, literature, or political—and covering all subject fields in music currently received by the Library of Congress and seven cooperating North American libraries.

*Arrangement:* Alphabetical by composer or author with added entries under subjects including see and see also references.

*Entries:* Composer or author, title, type of medium, publisher or record label with number, date, number of pages, illustrations, size, physical description of recording—speed, size, number of discs—series title, performers, author of program notes, subject headings, Library of Congress Classification number, Library of Congress catalog card number, code for contributing library.

*Special Features:* List of *Library of Congress Catalogs* in book form with sources and prices; elements of entries; entries also available in card form.

155. **Library Resources for Nurses: A Basic Collection for Supporting the Nursing Curriculum,** by Dale E. Shaffer, 437 Jennings Ave., Salem, OH 44460. 1973. $3. Order from author. 45p.

*Scope:* A selected bibliography of printed and audiovisual materials and equipment considered by the compiler to be "major resources particularly useful to the nursing student, and which should be considered for initial purchase when setting up a nursing program" (p.1). Criteria for inclusion in the collection are not given and the entries are not annotated. Types of materials included are: books, pamphlets, periodical indexes, periodicals and subscription agencies, filmstrips and major sources, filmloops and major sources, audiotapes and recordings, equipment and major sources. Included also is an estimate of the cost of the basic resources (itemized by type of material), an addendum of other nursing books in print, major sources of nursing books and pamphlets, and publications for the librarian.

*Arrangement:* By type of medium, then alphabetically by author or title.

*Entries:* Author (books), title, publisher/producer/distributor, date (books only), length in minutes/pages/number of items, price.

156. **List-O-Tapes; "All in One" Tape Catalog.** Trade Service Publications, Inc., 2720 Beverly Blvd., Los Angeles, CA 90057. Weekly. $60 annual subscription to loose-leaf weekly reports, including binder with tabs and current inserts.

*Scope:* Currently there are approximately 50,000 listings of prerecorded tape reels, cartridges, and cassettes in this loose-leaf catalog which is updated by a weekly service reporting releases as they are announced by manufacturers and recording companies. The catalog is divided into the following sections: New releases—the weekly reports showing releases for the week, pop titles, pop artists, classical titles, classical artists, composers (of classical composition), quad tapes, and 18 reference sections which index titles under such headings as bands, choral groups, Christmas, folk singers, guitar, Hawaiian, humorous, soundtrack and movie scores, spoken word, and others.

*Arrangement:* By categories listed above. Complete information appears in the title sections with cross references from the artist and composer entries.

*Entries:* Title of tape or collection, composer and type of composition (classical titles), artists/performers/musicians, instrument featured, tape system and speed symbol, label code, label number, other systems upon which same title is available, full contents if a collection.

*Special Features:* Loose-leaf format with 8½" x 11" pages in blue book-type binder; source directory and retail prices.

157. **Man and His Environment,** by Hannah C. Williams. Educational Film Library Association, 43 W. Sixty-first St., New York, NY 10023. 1972. $1 prepaid. 6p. (EFLA Service Supplement)

*Scope:* A list of 56 films selected on the basis of the evaluations of students, teachers, community leaders, and film librarians, as well as those involved in film production. An effort was made to include quality films that are short and accurate and which leave room for discussion. Subjects represented are ecological processes, geography, weather, geology, air, chemicals, energy, general pollution, noise, population, solid waste, water, wildlife, urbanization and industrialization, some solutions—city planning, resource management, teacher training. The films are suitable for elementary, high school, and adult audiences.

*Arrangement:* Alphabetical by title.

*Entries:* Title, running time, color or b/w, date, purchase price, distributor's name and address, audience level, descriptive-critical annotation.

*Special Features:* Subject index.

158. **Materials and Sources for Teaching the History of Books and Printing,** by Paul A. Winckler, Palmer Graduate Library School, Long Island University, C. W. Post Center, Greenvale, NY 11548. 1972. $1.65 check or money order payable to the author. 46p. (Reprinted from the *Journal of Education for Librarianship,* Summer and Fall issues, 1972)

*Scope:* A bibliographic essay which describes both printed and audiovisual materials, with "emphasis on those items which could be considered significant and of value in teaching a survey course in the history of books and printing" (Introduction to Part 1). The listing is designed primarily for the use of library educators, but could be of use also to library school students, librarians, historians, scholars, collectors, and bibliophiles. Divided into two parts, the first deals with printed works including general reference materials, bibliographies, general surveys of books and printing, surveys of the history of the printed book, paper and papermaking, binding, illustration, type and typography, the alphabet and writing, the book in the ancient world and in the medieval and modern world, origin of printing with movable type and incunabula, books and printing in America, and anthologies. The second essay lists films, filmstrips, and slides including sources, and comments on the production of slides, reproductions and realia, catalogs, sources for original materials, periodicals, special collections, special events and programs. There are comments on the value and use of the items included.

*Arrangement:* By categories mentioned above and/or by type of medium.

*Entries:* Title, author, producer/publisher, date if available, length, source, color or b/w, descriptive and critical comments.

159. **Materials for Metric Instruction,** compiled by Gary G. Bitter and Charles Geer. ERIC Information Analysis Center for Science, Mathematics and Environmental Education, The Ohio State University, Columbus, Ohio. Available from ERIC/SMEAC Information Reference Center, 1200 Chambers Road, 3rd Floor, Ohio State University, Columbus, OH 43212. 1975. $2. 85p. Available also in microfiche and hard copy from ERIC Document Reproduction Service, P.O. Box 190, Arlington, VA 22210. Apply for current prices. ED 115 488. (Mathematics Education Reports)

*Scope:* "This bibliography is intended as a quick reference or source of information for the teacher who is looking for supplementary metric materials other than books or workbooks" (Introduction). Included are entries for 41 metric kits, 8 task cards, 24 films, 36 filmstrips, 4 sets of slides, and 13 miscellaneous materials. No product evaluations are made and inclusion in the list does not imply endorsement of the product.

*Arrangement:* By type of medium, then randomly by title.

*Entries:* Title, author if any, date, distributor's name and address, purchase price as of March 1975, grade level, format, system, units, descriptive comments.

160. **A Materials Resource Guide for Teachers of Pre-School Children with Special Needs,** compiled by Ingrid Draper and others. The Detroit Pre-School Technical Assistance Resource and Training Center. Available from Physical Education and Recreation for the Handicapped: Information and Research Utilization Center (IRUC), 1201 Sixteenth St., N.W., Washington, DC 20036. 1976. $6.90 photocopy (no.237). 69p. Available also in microfiche and hard copy from ERIC Document Reproduction Service, P.O. Box 190, Arlington, VA 22210. Apply for current prices. ED 121 037.

*Scope:* "The *Materials Resource Guide* is not intended to provide an exhaustive collection of commercial materials. Rather, it should be looked upon as only a small sampling of available materials" (Introduction). Included are approximately 185 kits, games, picture sets, objects, printed materials, cassettes, filmstrips, records, and tapes in the following instructional areas: cognitive development, number concepts, perceptual motor development, language development, motor development sensory discrimination, self-awareness and socialization skills, and inservice training materials.

*Arrangement:* By instructional categories in the order listed above.

*Entries:* Type of material or title, number of items if a set or series, brief description, name of the publisher/producer.
*Special Features:* Directory of publishers.

161. **Media: An Annotated Catalogue of Law-Related Audio-Visual Materials,** edited by Susan E. Davison. Special Committee on Youth Education for Citizenship, American Bar Association, 1155 E. Sixtieth St., Chicago, IL 60637. 1975. $1. 79p. (Working Notes no.8) Available also in microfiche and hard copy from ERIC Document Reproduction Service, P.O. Box 190, Arlington, VA 22210. Apply for current prices. ED 107 553.

*Scope:* More than 400 films, filmstrips, audiocassettes, videotapes and mixed media kits are described in this catalog of law-related materials for elementary and secondary education. All of the items were reviewed by YEFC staff who "were particularly careful not to include those which were patently in error, or so out of date as to be misleading or confusing" (Introduction). The descriptions of contents were written primarily for the benefits of educators; annotations are intended to be descriptive rather than evaluative. The materials are grouped into seven major content areas: origins and basic concepts of law, the Constitution, the Bill of Rights, current issues, the political process, practical law, the teaching of law—sources and concepts. A section on drugs was not included because entire catalogs are devoted to that subject.
*Arrangement:* By subject categories listed above, then alphabetical by title.
*Entries:* Grade level, type of medium, guide if available, length in minutes, title and series title, distributor, producer, year of production, color or b/w, purchase and/or rental prices, descriptive annotation.
*Special Features:* Complete list of titles included in series; directory of distributors; index.

162. **Media Competency Training Materials, 1974–1975,** by Jacqueline M. Bolen and Donna Vander-Beugle. California Learning Resource Center, University of Southern California, 600 S. Commonwealth Ave., Los Angeles, CA 90005. Available in microfiche and hard copy from ERIC Document Reproduction Service, P.O. Box 190, Arlington, VA 22210. 1975. Apply for current prices. 326p. ED 114 055.

*Scope:* In compiling this catalog of print and nonprint training materials in the area of media competency skills the authors solicited information from over 500 education facilities and identified both locally produced and commercially published products. Subject areas are: bulletin boards, cassette tapes, computers and teaching machines, films, filmstrips and filmloops, flannelboards, operation of equipment, overhead projection, slides, transparencies, television, and videotape recordings. The materials are described but not evaluated.

*Arrangement:* By major categories of media, then alphabetical by title.

*Entries:* Title, producer, distributor, address, telephone number, free loan/purchase/rental price, media content area, media package format, equipment required, description of content.

163. **Media Evaluations 1976.** Indiana Association for Educational Communications and Technology, James E. Thompson, Executive Secretary, School of Education, Indiana State University, Terre Haute, IN 47809. 1976. $5. 45p.

*Scope:* An annotated list of 58 motion pictures, 110 series or individual filmstrip titles, and a "media mix" of 19 cassettes, recordings, kits, and 8mm filmloops—ranging from primary to adult levels—evaluated by the 1976 IAECT Media Evaluation Committee whose members are active media personnel or teachers in Indiana schools. The introduction explains that "each person evaluated the materials made available to him or her, usually in the process of evaluation for the local school" and that the evaluations are "opinions of the person evaluating the materials; no attempt was made to cover the field of new products." Copyright dates, when included, range from 1952 through 1975 with a majority of the titles produced during the 1970s. Ratings for each title or series range from excellent to poor and indicate whether or not purchase is recommended. Both fiction and nonfiction are included, the latter in broad subject classifications such as the arts, geography and history, library, literature, man in the universe, and technology.

*Arrangement:* Divided into three main sections: films, filmstrips, and media mix. Each section is divided by broad Dewey Decimal Classification numbers (100s, 300s, 500s, etc.) and titles are listed randomly under these numbers.

*Entries:* Title or series title, type of medium and number of titles if a series, color, running time, copyright date when available, distributor or producer, sales price, 25–145 word descriptive/critical annotation including titles of individual filmstrips in a series, grade level, rating, recommendation concerning purchase, initials of evaluator.

*Special Features:* List of active members of the IAECT Media Evaluation Committee; evaluation form used for audiovisual materials; addresses of sources; title index.

164. **Media Review Digest: The Only Complete Guide to Reviews of Non-Book Media,** edited by C. Edward Wall, B. Penny Northern, and Cynthia Rigg. 1970–date. Annual in 2 parts in hard cover with annual subject indexes to each part and paperback supplements to each part included in the subscription price. Entries in the supplements are subsequently merged with additional citations gathered during the entire year to form the basis for the next annual volume. Pierian Press, 5000 Washtenaw Ave., Ann Arbor, MI 48104. 1973/74. $65; 1974/75. $65; 1975/76. $79.60. (Successor to *Multi-Media Reviews Index.* 1970. $19.50; 1971. $29.50; 1972. $35)

*Scope:* A comprehensive index to reviews on all subjects in over 200 periodicals with more than 50,000 review citations per year. Part 1 covers educational 16mm films, feature films, videotapes, filmstrips, and miscellaneous formats; part 2 indexes reviews of popular, classical, and spoken word records and tapes. In both parts primary emphasis is on educational, instructional, and informational media. Parts are available separately or combined.

*Arrangement:* Main text of part 1 is divided into three sections by type of medium with title entries listed alphabetically under each medium; part 2, record and tape section, is alphabetical by performer, composer, or author.

*Entries:* Part 1—title or series title, producer/distributor, country of origin, release date, size (mm), length in minutes/frames, sound or silent, color or b/w, brief description of content, subject headings, Dewey Decimal Classification number, audience level, evaluation symbols, review source(s). Part 2—composer/author, title, date, artist(s), performer(s), disc/tape/cassette, length, label and number, review rating, evaluation source.

*Special Features:* Introductions to parts 1 and 2 (purpose, explanation of scope, arrangement, review sources, ratings, future developments, acknowledgements, etc.) followed by a key to abbreviations and list of periodicals and review services indexed; list of film awards and prizes; list of record awards and prizes; mediagraphies; subject indexes in supplements; separate indexes in supplements; separate indexes and lists of producers and distributors.

165. **Medieval and Renaissance Music on Long-Playing Records: Supplement, 1962–1971,** by James Coover and Richard Colvig. Information Coordinators, Inc., 1435–37 Randolph St., Detroit, MI 48226. 1973. $8.50; $7 paper. 285p. (Detroit Studies in Music Bibliography). (Continues the authors' *Medieval and Renaissance Music on Long-Playing Records,* and *First Supplement 1960–1961*)

*Scope:* Covers a decade of newly issued and reissued anthologies of Medieval and Renaissance music recorded in Great Britain, France, Italy, Germany, and the United States. All records are 12″, 33⅓ rpm unless otherwise noted. In some cases, two or more issues are given; these may represent foreign and domestic issues of the same recording, monaural and stereophonic issues, or successive numbers released by the same company.

*Arrangement:* The Chant list is arranged by place name or by the name of an institution with which the performing group is associated. Anthologies are alphabetical by title, or by performer or performing group when no title could be determined.

*Entries:* Album title or place name/institution, performer(s), conductor, instrument(s), record label and number, individual titles and composers.

*Special Features:* Addenda and Corrigenda to Original Edition and First Supplement; Index to Anthologies and Individual Discographies by Composer; Performer Index.

166. **Meet Some of Your Four Billion Neighbors at a Film Festival: One Phase of the Project Neighbors Unlimited.** Association for Childhood Education International, 3615 Wisconsin Ave., N.W., Washington, DC 20016. 1974. 50¢. 14p.

*Scope:* In 1973 a large number of people were asked by the International-Intercultural Education Committee of the ACEI to submit titles of outstanding films on international and intercultural themes. Among the more than 70 titles suggested, previewed, and evaluated by the committee, 24 were selected for showing at a film festival and are listed in this leaflet. Most of the films are considered by the committee to be suitable for elementary school children; 4 are especially suitable for use with teachers; and all of the titles are considered to be enlightening, outstanding, and provocative.

*Arrangement:* Alphabetical by title.

*Entries:* Title, color or b/w, running time, producer/distributor, date, descriptive/critical annotation suggesting suitable uses and age levels.

*Special Features:* Addresses of producers, distributors, and organizations.

167. **The Metric System: A Bibliography of Instructional Materials,** compiled by Karen G. Beam. 2d rev. ed. Published jointly by the Metropolitan School District of Wayne Township and the Indiana Department of Public Instruction, Indianapolis, IN 46204. 1975. 36p. Avail-

able in microfiche and hard copy from ERIC Document Reproduction
Service, P.O. Box 190, Arlington, VA 22210. Apply for current prices.
ED 104 718.

*Scope:* Designed as an awareness tool, not an evaluative selection
guide, the materials included are books, duplicating masters,
periodicals, U.S. Government documents, charts, 8mm films,
16mm films, filmstrips, games, multimedia kits, realia, posters,
recordings, slides, and transparencies concerned with the metric
system. It is emphasized in the preface that inclusion in the list
does not constitute an endorsement; appropriateness of the materials must be judged "on the basis of the needs of the specific
learners under consideration."

*Arrangement:* By type of medium, then alphabetical by author or
title.

*Entries:* Author (books), title or series title, grade level, brief description, publisher/producer/distributor, date, length in minutes/
pages/number of items, color (films), catalog order number, pur-
chase/rental prices.

*Special Features:* Addresses of producers.

168. **Mexican Americans: Resources to Build Cultural Understanding,** by
Lois B. Jordan. Libraries Unlimited, Inc., P.O. Box 263, Littleton,
CO 80120. 1973. $10. 216p.

*Scope:* A selected, annotated bibliography of 1,028 titles of books,
films, filmstrips, 8mm filmloops, recordings, slides, transparencies,
and other media in English which provide information about the
current problems, the historical background, and cultural heritage
of Mexican Americans and which are suitable for college and high
school students, plus some materials for the junior high school age
group. The media were published or produced during the years
1949–72, but emphasis has been placed on materials issued since
1962.

*Arrangement:* Printed materials, part 1, is subdivided into Mexico's
history, Mexican Americans in the United States, the arts, literature, biography, fiction, and further subdivided by periods and
subjects; within categories, the books are listed alphabetically by
author. Audiovisual materials, part 2, is divided by type of medium, then arranged alphabetically by title.

*Entries:* Identification number, title, size, length or number of
frames/slides/discs, speed (for records), producer/distributor,
date, color or b/w, descriptive annotation. Book entries include
author, title, complete bibliographic information, and annotation.

*Special Features:* Author, title, and subject indexes; Appendix A, Distinguished Mexican American Personalities; Appendix B, Mexican American Organizations; Appendix C, Chicano Press Association, Periodicals and Newspapers of Interest to the Mexican American; Appendix D, General Reference, Bibliographies, Directories, Guides, Handbooks.

169. **Motion Pictures in the Audiovisual Archives Division of the National Archives,** by Mayfield S. Bray and William T. Murphy. National Archives and Records Service, Washington, DC 20408. Available in microfiche and hard copy from ERIC Document Reproduction Service, P.O. Box 190, Arlington, VA 22210. 1972. Apply for current prices. 37p. ED 081 241.

*Scope:* Over 60,000 reels of edited and unedited films dating from 1894 are contained in the National Archives collection and are described in this paper. The materials are in the form of out-takes, newsreels, information and training films, feature films, and documentaries. Individual researchers may study films in the motion picture research room, and groups may view them in the National Archives Theater. There is no charge for screening, but reservations are generally needed. Reproduction services are available for filmmakers and other users, except for films encumbered by copyright and/or other restrictions. Although no loan service is available, government films that are in current circulation may be rented or purchased through the National Audiovisual Center, Washington, DC 20409.

*Arrangement:* By federal government agency.

*Entries:* Name of agency, film number, date, number of reels, description of content.

*Special Features:* General index to agencies, subjects, personal names, and places.

170. **Movies for Kids: A Guide for Parents and Teachers on the Entertainment Film for Children 9–13,** by Edith Zornow and Ruth M. Goldstein. Avon Books, 959 Eighth Ave., New York, NY 10019. 1973. $1.65. 224p.

*Scope:* A selection of 300 critically annotated features and short films, all available in 16mm, for rental and sale, for nontheatrical showings to sub-teens in homes, schools, churches, camps, clubs, and libraries. Selections are based on overall quality and entertainment value.

*Arrangement:* By category—feature films, a supplementary list of features "not prime but choice," short films—then alphabetical by title.

*Entries:* Title, producer, date, length, color or b/w, credits (cast, direction, designs, costuming, editing, lyrics, music, photography, special effects), distributor code, descriptive/critical annotation.

*Special Features:* How to look at movies; addresses of film distributors; 100 books about movies; recommended film periodicals; a selection of stills from feature films.

171. **A Multimedia Approach to Children's Literature: A Selective List of Films, Filmstrips, and Recordings Based on Children's Books,** edited by Ellin Green and Madalynne Schoenfeld. American Library Association, 50 E. Huron St., Chicago, IL 60611. 1972. $4. 262p.

*Scope:* Approximately 425 books, 175 16mm films, 175 silent and sound filmstrips, and 300 long-playing discs and tape cassettes released before July 1, 1971, are included in this "buying guide to a quality collection of book-related nonprint materials to use with children from preschool to grade eight" (Preface). Types of literature represented are picture books, traditional and folk literature, literary fairy tales, fiction, dramatic arts, poetry and song, and some background books on illustrators and authors of children's books. A section preceding the main text lists related readings, selection aids, program aids, realia, figurines, stuffed animals, and portfolios of posters useful in storytelling and book programs.

*Arrangement:* Alphabetical by book title followed by titles of films, filmstrips and recordings related to each book.

*Entries:* Type of medium, title, producer, date, producer's serial number, size, speed, length in minutes/frames, color or b/w, rental/sales price, grade level, distributor, annotation.

*Special Features:* Indexes to authors, film titles, filmstrip titles, media about or presented by authors and illustrators, record titles, and subjects; Directory of Distributors.

172. **Multimedia for Americanization Programs.** Bureau of Continuing Education Curriculum Development, The State Education Department, Albany, NY 12224. Available in microfiche and hard copy from ERIC Document Reproduction Service, P.O. Box 190, Arlington, VA 22210. 1973. Apply for current prices. 110p. ED 077 205.

*Scope:* A selected, annotated compilation of videotapes, records, tapes, filmstrips, films, filmloops, transparencies, charts, and kits recommended for use in Americanization programs. All of the materials included were previewed. Divided into 2 parts, part 1 is concerned with the learning of the English language, while part 2 lists materials on the following subjects: citizenship, home and school, community, American culture, resources of the United States, American system of government, geography of the United

States and of the state of New York, major events and trends in the making of America, twentieth-century America, and current American affairs.

*Arrangement:* By main subject categories in the order listed above, then by type of medium.

*Entries:* Type of medium, title, producer, date, length in minutes/number of items, sound or silent, color or b/w, source in code, availability, annotation, level of difficulty in code.

*Special Features:* Producer/distributor code; alphabetical list of producers/distributors; "Message to the Instructor"; "Using Audiovisual Equipment."

173. **Multimedia Materials for Teaching Young Children; A Bibliography of Multi-Cultural Resources,** by Harry A. Johnson. University of Connecticut, Storrs, CN 06268. Available in microfiche and hard copy from ERIC Document Reproduction Service, P.O. Box 190, Arlington, VA 22210. 1972. Apply for current prices. 27p. ED 088 578.

*Scope:* A descriptive, evaluative list of predominantly audiovisual materials plus 50 selected books for teaching young children about our multi-cultural society. The nonbook materials are 16mm films, 8mm filmloops, filmstrips, recordings, audiotapes, photographs, study prints, and multimedia kits.

*Arrangement:* By type of medium then alphabetical by title—except books which are alphabetical by author.

*Entries:* Author (books), title or series title, color or b/w, length in minutes/frames/pages/items, publisher/distributor, order number, grade level, individual titles if a series or set, purchase/rental prices, descriptive/evaluative annotation.

*Special Features:* List of producers and distributors.

174. **Museum Media,** by Paul Wasserman and Esther Herman. Gale Research Co., Book Tower, Detroit, MI 48226. 1973. $62. 455p.

*Scope:* A comprehensive directory and index to publications and audiovisual materials available from 732 United States and Canadian producers "intended to provide bibliographic control of books, booklets, monographs, catalogs, pamphlets and leaflets, films and filmstrips, slides, and other media prepared and distributed by museums and art galleries" (Preface). Excluded are magazines, journals, and newsletters. Some of the subjects included are: archaeology, art, botanical gardens, horticulture, monuments and memorials, natural history, paleontology, planetaria, history, and zoology. Although planned as a biennial publication, a new edition has not been announced.

*Arrangement:* Alphabetical by institution, then type of medium, then alphabetical by title.

*Entries:* Name and address of institution, ordering information, type of medium, title, author, date, size, length (pages/minutes/frames), illustrations, color or b/w, sound or silent, price/rental fee, distributor, terms of availability.

*Special Features:* Title and key word index of media; institutions grouped by broad subject fields in which they produce media; geographical index of institutions.

175. **National Center for Audio Tapes 1974–76 Catalog.** National Center for Audio Tapes, Stadium Building, Boulder, CO 80302. 1974–76. $2 within United States; $3 to foreign countries. 340p. *Supplement.* Free. 16p.

*Scope:* Approximately 14,000 tapes in the main volume selected on the basis of curricular relevance and production quality which can be rerecorded for any individual, group, educational institution, or business firm provided that the restrictions are adhered to. Subject areas include: the arts—general, architecture, dance, drama, graphic art, handicrafts, design, music, painting, photography, printing, sculpture; education—history, theory and practice, media, special areas of education; language and literature; mathematics and science—mathematics, biological sciences, chemistry, physics, geology, meteorology, astronomy, medicine, space exploration; physical and recreational activities; social science—history, economics, political science, sociology, anthropology, geography, philosophy, religion, psychology, military history and civil defense; vocational and technical fields—agriculture, business, consumer guidance and home management, engineering, trades. Policies, procedures, and fees which govern availability and use are given.

*Arrangement:* (1) Alphabetical by program title; (2) Subject Index, by broad subject headings with individual titles and title numbers under subheadings; (3) Numeric Index with series titles and numbers, and individual titles and numbers.

*Entries:* Series title, series stock number, producer, broadcast restrictions, grade level, individual title, individual title stock number, series description, running time.

*Special Features:* General information on arrangement of catalog; purchasing information; producer index.

176. **National Directory of Safety Films, 1975–76.** National Safety Council, 425 N. Michigan Ave., Chicago, IL 60611. 1975. $4.50. 58p.

*Scope:* More than 1,000 16mm films, 8mm films, and sound filmstrips covering safety in areas of industry, motor transportation, traffic, home, farm, public, and school.

*Arrangement:* Alphabetical by title under broad subject categories.

*Entries:* Title, producer, sponsors, distributors, screening time, silent or sound, color or b/w, television clearance, information about purchase or loan, descriptive annotation of 10–40 words.

*Special Features:* Title index; guide to film sources.

177. **A National State of the Art Study of Curriculum Instructional Materials for Distributive Education,** by Marvin Hirshfeld and Jerome I. Leventhal. Division of Vocational Education, Temple University, Philadelphia, PA 19140. Available in microfiche and hard copy from ERIC Document Reproduction Service, P.O. Box 190, Arlington, VA 22210. 1973. Apply for current prices. 2v. ED 105 195; ED 105 196.

*Scope:* Provides a partial listing of books, slides, films, tapes, records, transparencies, booklets, and kits available for curriculum and instructional enrichment in distributive education. The grouping of all materials is according to the U.S. Office of Education Classification of Instructional Programs for Distributive Education. The subjects included are: advertising services, apparel and accessories, automotive, finance and credit, floristry, food distribution, food services, general merchandise, hardware, building materials, farm and garden supplies and equipment, home furnishings, hotel and lodging, industrial marketing, insurance, international trade, personal services, real estate, recreation and tourism, transportation, other retail trade, and other instructional programs.

*Arrangement:* By subject areas, then by type of medium, then alphabetical by title.

*Entries:* Title, author (print), name and address of publisher/producer/distributor, date if available, cost, length in pages/minutes/frames/items, teacher or student material, grade level, suggested time of use, objectives, summary description, available instructional material and tests if any.

178. **New Instructional Materials for Agricultural Education 1976,** prepared by the Curriculum Materials Committee, Agricultural Education Division of the American Vocational Association, 1510 H St., N.W., Washington, DC 20005. 1976. Free. 37p. Published annually. Supply limited.

*Scope:* A selected list of 249 titles including sets of slides, transparencies, filmstrips, printed guides and manuals currently available for use by teachers of vocational agriculture, agricultural supervisors and teacher educators. All of the materials were developed by persons engaged in vocational education in agriculture; the materials have not been distributed commercially; they were developed during the past year and have not been listed in previous editions of *New Instructional Materials;* they are considered to be of interest and use beyond the boundary of the state in which they were prepared; they are available from the source, or if not, are available through the ERIC system and/or AIM-ARM. Subjects included are: field crops, horticulture, forestry, animal science, soils, diseases and pests, agricultural engineering, agricultural economics, agricultural occupations, professional, and teacher education. The materials are described, evaluated, and classified by the AGDEX filing system.

*Arrangement:* By AGDEX numbers and the subjects listed above.

*Entries:* Title, AGDEX number, date, medium or format, length in number of pages/slides/transparencies/frames, source code number, description of content, free/price/availability information.

*Special Features:* Sources of instructional materials.

179. **The New Listener's Companion and Record Guide,** by B. H. Haggin. 4th ed. Horizon Press, 156 Fifth Ave., New York, NY 10010. 1974. $10 cloth; $4.95 paperback. 399p.

*Scope:* Divided into two parts, the first half of the book is a discussion of the meaning of music, musical procedures and forms, and a critical survey of the works of all of the great composers of the eighteenth, nineteenth, and twentieth centuries, the music of earlier centuries, American music, and jazz. The second half of the volume is a critically annotated discography in which the author discusses in detail what he considers to be good recordings of works mentioned in the first half so that his readers may be made "aware of things in the music which they mightn't notice by themselves" (Introduction).

*Arrangement:* First half, by topics, composers and/or centuries. Discography, in two parts: recorded performances of the past, listed under names of performers or names of collections; recorded performances of today, listed under names of composers or names of performers (collections), or titles of records.

*Entries:* Performer, composer, title of collection, titles of individual works, record labels and numbers, critical commentary about each issue and performance.

*Special Features:* Early chapters addressed to beginning listeners; general index; index to performers; additional recorded performances issued through 1973.

180. **NICEM Update of Nonbook Media.** National Information Center for Educational Media, University of Southern California, University Park, Los Angeles, CA 90007. 1977. Issued every other year in 4 bimonthly supplements. Provided without cost to purchasers of 5 or more NICEM *Indexes.* 4v.

*Scope:* This multimedia catalog supplements the 14 basic NICEM *Indexes;* like them, it is generated from the NICEM data bank at the University of Southern California and covers the same 26 broad subjects. Audience levels range from preschool through college and adult. Types of educational media included are: 16mm films, filmstrips, 8mm motion cartridges, audiotapes, videotapes, overhead transparencies, records, slides.

*Arrangement:* Main section, the "Alphabetical Guide," is arranged by type of medium followed by individual titles together with series titles arranged alphabetically; the section entitled "Subject Guide" is divided into 26 broad subject headings and numerous subheadings arranged alphabetically, followed by type of medium, then, alphabetical by title.

*Entries:* Main section—title or series/album title, description of format, length in minutes/frames/records, stock or color code, description of content, audience or grade level, producer and distributor codes, year of release, individual titles if a series/album with minutes/frames for each, Library of Congress catalog card number, broadcast quality (videotapes).

*Special Features:* "How to Use This Index," "Subject Heading Outline," "Index to Subject Headings," "Directory of Producers and Distributors," part 1, arranged alphabetically by code and including addresses; part 2, arranged alphabetically by name.

181. **Nonfiction Film: A Critical History,** by Richard Meran Barsam. E. P. Dutton & Co., Inc., 201 Park Ave., S., New York, NY 10003. 1973. $9.95; $4.95 paper. 332p.

*Scope:* In this history, which covers the period 1920–70, the quality, significance, and value of 155 nonfiction films are discussed and reference is made to many additional titles. Nonfiction and documentary film definitions are quoted in the introductory sections. In the historical discussion, the author emphasizes films produced in the United States and Great Britain and includes only those early European films which have had a direct influence on the development of British and American nonfiction filmmaking. The author omits discussion of nonfiction films of the United States Information Agency, the National Film Board of Canada, and

UNESCO, as well as films made for television because "they have been covered in other recent studies" (Introduction). Types of nonfiction films are, according to the author, documentaries, factual films, travel films, educational/training and classroom films, newsreels, animated or cartoon films. Among the well-known filmmakers whose works are included are: John Grierson, Robert Flaherty, Basil Wright, Joris Ivens, Pare Lorentz, Paul Rotha, Frank Capra, Richard Leacock, D. A. Pennebaker, and Frederick Wiseman. The book is illustrated with photographs from some of the films.

*Arrangement:* Chronological, 1920–70.

*Entries:* Main text includes title, filmmaker, credits, date, and critical discussion. Appendix A includes title, date, country, running time, distributor, main production credits.

*Special Features:* Photographic illustrations; major nonfiction and documentary awards; bibliography; index.

182. **NRMA's Retail Training Film Directory.** Rev. ed. Personnel Group, National Retail Merchants Association, 100 W. Thirty-first St., New York, NY 10001. 1975. $8, members; $12.50, nonmembers. 76p.

*Scope:* More than 200 films covering a wide variety of subjects and intended as an aid in training retail employees. Subject headings include: home furnishings, ready-to-wear and accessories, men's wear and men's furnishings, textiles, customer relations, safety, sales training, management development, office and restaurant store operations, supervisory training, retail careers, human relations.

*Arrangement:* Alphabetical by subject areas and then alphabetical by title.

*Entries:* Title, distributor, type of medium, running time, 10–60-word descriptive annotation, borrowing/renting/buying terms.

*Special Features:* Descriptions of the characteristics of the visual training aids included in the Directory; guidelines for selecting training aids and preparing the presentation; title index; distributor index.

183. **Opera Recordings: A Critical Guide,** by Kenn Harris. Drake Publishers, Inc., 381 Park Ave., S., New York, NY 10016. 1973. $9.95. 328p.

*Scope:* "This book should serve two purposes. One is, through the listing of all available recordings of each of the 76 operas covered herein, to inform the reader of each of his possible choices. The second and principal one is, through the evaluations of many if not all of these recordings, to give the reader an idea of which of these recordings he should own and for what reasons" (Preface). All of the complete recordings of the opera under discussion which were available at press time are listed at the beginning of each article, but not all of these are evaluated in the text which follows. The recordings chosen for evaluation are those considered by the author to be distinguished or at least important due to one or more artists in the cast.

*Arrangement:* Alphabetical by opera titles.

*Entries:* Title, composer, major artist(s), orchestra and conductor, number of discs, label(s) and label number(s), (United States and United Kingdom if available), critical reviews.

**Special Features:** Index.

184. **Oral History Collections,** compiled and edited by Alan M. Meckler and Ruth McMullin. R. R. Bowker Co., 1180 Avenue of the Americas, New York, NY 10036. 1975. $29.50. 344p.

*Scope:* A comprehensive annotated index to thousands of interviews in collections located at several hundred oral history centers, libraries, and archives in the United States and selected foreign countries: Canada, Israel, Ireland, United Kingdom. "The names of those whose memoirs are included comprises a list of the people most active in recent and contemporary history" (Foreword).

*Arrangement:* In two parts: a name and subject index, and a section which lists U.S. and foreign oral history centers. These two sections complement each other and must be used together for the most complete information. The name and subject index headings are alphabetical; within subjects, the materials are alphabetical by the oral history center which appears in italics, and then by project title, if necessary. The U.S. Oral History Centers section and Foreign Oral History Centers section are alphabetical by state or country, and within each, alphabetical by center. See and see also references are included in both sections.

*Entries:* Name and subject index: name, title or position of person, number of pages if interview has been transcribed, name of collection in which interview took place, conditions under which interview may be available for use, language if not English, number of hours of tape, date of interview, name of center(s) where located, reference to a related interview, state or country in which the center is located. Section which lists U.S. and foreign oral history centers: name, address, general information, accessibility, purpose of the program.

*Special Features:* The foreword gives background information about the oral history movement in this country and describes the methodology used for the preparation of this volume.

185. **People: Annotated Multiethnic Bibliography K-12,** compiled by Delores Gilmore and Kenneth Petrie. Evaluation and Selection Division, Department of Educational Media and Technology, Montgomery County Public Schools, Rockville, MD 20850. 1973. Apply. 344p. Available also in microfiche and hard copy from ERIC Document Reproduction Service, P.O. Box 190, Arlington, VA 22210. Apply for current prices. ED 099 864.

*Scope:* In addition to a wide selection of printed materials and sources of information, the list includes approximately 220 titles of cassettes, filmstrips, filmloops, records, tapes, transparencies, and multimedia kits about ethnic groups in America. The work is divided into eight sections: Asian Americans, Jewish Americans, Mexican Americans, Native Americans, Puerto Rican Americans, other hyphenated Americans, all Americans (multiethnic), and late entries. The list complements four earlier bibliographies on Negroes in American life. Grade levels are included and entries are annotated except in cases where the title is self-explanatory.
*Arrangement:* By categories in the order mentioned above, then by subheadings followed by titles in alphabetical order.
*Entries:* Title, author (printed materials), type of medium (nonprint), publisher/producer/distributor, date, price, grade level, annotation, asterisk denoting nonprint title.
*Special Features:* Title index.

186. **Phonolog: The All-In-One Record Reporter.** Phonolog Publishing Division, Trade Service Publications, Inc., 2720 Beverly Blvd., Los Angeles, CA 90057. Weekly. 1948 to date. $162 annual subscription to loose-leaf weekly reports and replacement sheets; $38.50 for complete accumulation of current inserts and *Phonolog* stand (available only with annual subscription)

*Scope:* Currently there are over 6,000 loose-leaf 8½" x 11" punched pages in this catalog, which includes more than 1,000,000 separate listings of long-playing, extended play, 78 rpm and 45 rpm recordings of all types of music. The catalog is divided into the following sections: pop titles, pop artists, pop albums, classical titles, classical artists, classical composers, plus 10 reference sections which index titles in the popular section under these headings: band, Christmas albums and singles, children's, Hawaiian, Latin-American, motion pictures, sacred, show tunes, specialties and miscellaneous, theme songs. The information is updated in three parts: triweekly inserts covering over 500 record producers; a weekly card service listing all of the albums and single records reported to *Phonolog* for release each week; Top Hits, a counter card published every two weeks—compiled from a survey of singles and albums which are currently in popular favor.

*Arrangement:* By categories listed above. Complete information appears in title sections, with cross references from the artist and composer entries.

*Entries:* Title, composer and type of composition (classical titles), artists/performers/musicians, distributor, title of album and contents, label code, label number, type and speed of record.

*Special Features:* Loose-leaf format and 12-section steel desk rack on turntable; popular music sections printed on buff-colored paper, classical sections on blue paper; addresses of major producers.

187. **A Practical Guide to Urban & Environmental Movies (Educational Orientation),** by Ambrose Klain and Dennis M. Phelan. Rev. ed. Council of Planning Librarians, P.O. Box 229, Monticello, IL 61856. 1975. $5. 49p. (Exchange Bibliography no.780)

*Scope:* A list of urban and environmental 16mm films, intended primarily as a guide to college instructors. Materials are presented in tabular sample teaching schedules for 10-week terms and for 16-week semesters. Entries are not evaluated.

*Arrangement:* In eight tables, listing individual film titles by weeks in the schedule, and by series titles (Table VIII).

*Entries:* Title, date, running time, distributor, rental cost, order number.

*Special Features:* Alphabetical title list of the films with descriptions from distributors' catalogs; distributors and sources.

188. **Programmed Instruction in Librarianship: A Classified Bibliography of Programmed Texts and Other Materials,** by Henry M. Yaple. *Occasional Papers,* Publications Office, 249 Armory Building, Graduate School of Library Science, University of Illinois, Champaign, IL 61820. 1976. $2 prepaid, check payable to University of Illinois. 25p. (*Occasional Papers* no.124)

*Scope:* A comprehensive list of programs produced between 1960 and 1974, designed to teach students at various levels about almost all aspects of the library. The basic criterion for inclusion was that the material be some kind of self-paced instructional sequence concerned with library education. Films are not included because they are not self-paced sequences. Examples of materials included are: numerous slide/tape presentations which are designed to orient college students to their libraries, sequences to train clerical employees in library methods, a number of programs which teach cataloging and classification, an on-line computer assisted program to instruct librarians in the use of MEDLINE, a program to teach Russian to librarians, and a computer-assisted instructional program to train elementary school students to locate information in periodicals. Most of the entries are not annotated.

*Arrangement:* Alphabetical by library education curriculum areas, then alphabetical by author.

*Entries:* Author, title, publisher/producer, place, date, name and date of periodical if an article, price, length in minutes/number of slides/pages/frames, EDRS prices and ED number if in ERIC, intended audience.

*Special Features:* List of bibliographies on programmed instruction; the author's Vita.

189. **Programmed Learning and Individually Paced Instruction: Bibliography,** by Carl H. Hendershot. Sponsored by the National Society for Programmed Instruction. 5th ed. Available from Carl H. Hendershot, 1414 Ridgewood Dr., Bay City, MI 48706. 1973. $37 loose-leaf in vinyl binder with index. 2v. Basic *Bibliography* with *Supplements One and Two.* 1975. $53; Basic *Bibliography* with *Supplements One, Two, Three and Four.* Through 1976. $63 including v.2 binder.

*Scope:* Current sources of individualized instruction in 230 subjects and descriptions of programs and devices designed for self-study or for students in elementary, secondary, college, professional, paraprofessional, vocational, trades, industry, business, adult and basic education programs.

*Arrangement:* Divided into sections. Section A, the main section, is an alphabetical list of subjects with program titles included under appropriate headings; Section B is arranged alphabetically by publisher with titles under names of their publishers; Section C lists instructional systems under names of publishers; Section D describes the machines and is arranged alphabetically by manufacturer; Section E is a list of resources and references about programmed instruction.

*Entries:* Subject, title, author, approximate hours, level, number of pages/frames, publisher, cost, availability, machine or device, brief descriptive note indicating prerequisites, possible uses, teacher's manual, tests.

*Special Features:* Directory of publishers and manufacturers; instruction written in languages other than English; publishers from countries other than the United States and Canada; vinyl binder with index.

190. **Protocol Catalog: Materials for Teacher Education.** 3d ed. Florida State Department of Education, Tallahassee, FL 32302. Available in microfiche and hard copy from ERIC Document Reproduction Service, P.O. Box 190, Arlington, VA 22210. 1974. Apply for current prices. 30p. ED 090 215.

*Scope:* A list of 129 films, filmstrips, audiocassettes and videotapes dealing with the concept of protocols—produced at 13 universities and education centers. Protocol materials as defined in this catalog are instructional media that reproduce the behavior of children and others in a variety of settings for purposes of study and analysis. The six subject categories included are: curriculum and instruction, educational psychology, language, literature, reading, and social foundations.

*Arrangement:* Alphabetical by title.

*Entries:* Number, title, concept name, brief description of content, producer code, grade level of students appearing in the medium (not level of use), type of medium, color or b/w, manual if available, running time, rental/purchase prices.

*Special Features:* Titles indexed according to the six categories mentioned above; additional materials complementary to the concept of protocols; sources and addresses.

191. **The Psychology Teacher's Resource Book: First Course.** The American Psychological Association, 1200 Seventeenth St., N.W., Washington, DC 20036. 1973. $3. 179p.

*Scope:* As a service to teachers of precollege psychology, the Association staff prepared this comprehensive compilation of bibliographies and reviews; many of the latter were contributed on a continuing basis for publication in the newsletter, *Periodically,* by a network of reviewers known to be interested in precollege psychology. The categories of materials included are: introductory textbooks, books of readings, laboratory manuals, periodicals for the high school, novels and case studies, biographies and other popular books, audiovisual materials, reference materials, equipment and supplies. The audiovisual section includes film catalogs, film series, television courses, slide sets and transparencies, audio catalogs and a topical listing of films and filmstrips. Subjects included in the latter are: communication and language, emotions and motivation, growth and development, learning and testing, mental deficiency, personality development, psychology as a science, psychotherapy, sense organs and the nervous system, social and antisocial behavior, and statistics. The entries in the film and filmstrip section are not annotated; they were selected because they were suggested by program members or editors, seemed timeless, and/or had late copyright dates.

*Arrangement:* By categories of media and subjects in the order listed above.

*Entries:* Author (books), title, publisher/producer/distributor, date, length in minutes/pages/frames, color or b/w, price (printed materials), reviews or brief descriptions for entries in some sections.

*Special Features:* Abbreviations and addresses of distributors; equipment, animals, and supplies; addresses of national organizations; "Some Ways of Increasing Student Involvement"; "Some Ways of Organizing Instruction"; "Comments"; publishers' addresses; author index.

192. **Railroad Film Directory,** compiled by the Association of American Railroads, American Railroads Building, Washington, DC 20036. 14th ed. 1976. Apply. 46p. Frequently revised.

*Scope:* Motion pictures and filmstrips which feature the history, physical properties, operations, and accomplishments of the railroads, as well as a few of the classic Hollywood productions involving railroads. Approximately 165 titles.

*Arrangement:* Alphabetical by title under type of medium with subject index.

*Entries:* Title, date, distributor and producer, running time, silent or sound, color or b/w, availability on free or rental basis, television clearance, narrative phonorecords or study guides if any, descriptive annotation.

*Special Features:* Address list of distributors; subject index.

193. **La Raza in Films: A List of Films and Filmstrips,** compiled by Cynthia Baird. Latin American Library, 1457 Fruitvale Ave., Oakland, CA 94601. 1972. Free. 68p.

*Scope:* A selected list of 9 filmstrips, 6 8mm films, and 240 16mm films, with brief descriptions or critical evaluations. "Originally intended to include only so-called 'Chicano films,' it now encompasses films and filmstrips on the great pre-Columbian civilizations of the American continents, the Spanish conquest and domination, modern Latin America (excluding Brazil), Spanish-speaking minorities in the United States, and the relatively new Third World concept of Latin America" (Introduction).

*Arrangement:* By subject category, then alphabetical by title under type of medium.

*Entries:* Title, color or b/w, length, language, purchase price, distributor/producer, annotation.

*Special Features:* Bibliography; directory of film producers and distributors.

194. **Recent Materials on China and U.S.-China Relations: An Annotated Bibliography,** by Robert Goldberg. Service Center for Teachers of Asian Studies, Association for Asian Studies, Ohio State University, 29 W. Woodruff Ave., Columbus, OH 43210. Franklin R. Buchanan, Director. 1974. $1. 32p. Available also in microfiche and hard copy from ERIC Document Reproduction Service, P.O. Box 190, Arlington, VA 22210. Apply for current prices. ED 109 002. (Service Center Papers on Asian Studies, no.8)

*Scope:* The purpose of this bibliographic essay of books, articles, and audiovisual materials on China is to help educators identify new materials most suitable for classroom and community programs "and to discuss some of the emerging themes in America's new relationship with China . . . around which discussions may be organized" (Introduction). The essay is in six parts: accounts by recent visitors to China, general books about China and U.S.-China relations, major areas of professional interest in China, important issues in Sino-American relations, Chinese periodicals/Chinese perspectives, resources for teachers. Most of the materials date from 1971–74.

*Arrangement:* In six sections in the order listed above, subdivided by specific subject headings and by type of medium.

*Entries:* Author, title, periodical/publisher/producer, address, date, length in pages/minutes/number of tapes/records/cassettes, price, individual titles if a series or set, brief annotation, asterisk denoting highly recommended title.

195. **Recommended East Asian Core Collections for Children's, High School, Public, Community College, and Undergraduate College Libraries,** edited by William H. O. Scott, Wilson Library, West Washington State College, Bellingham, WA 98225; compiled by the East Asian Bibliographic Group. Available in microfiche and hard copy from ERIC Document Reproduction Service, P.O. Box 190, Arlington, VA 22210. 1974. Apply for current prices. 196p. ED 110 021.

*Scope:* A basic buying list for libraries seeking to develop their Far East holdings, this work resulted from the efforts of librarians, faculty, and students in East Asian Studies from throughout the northwestern United States who organized the East Asian Bibliographic Group and conceived the project at conferences held in 1972 and again in 1973. "The core collections include materials which the pooled judgment of participants consider as either the best, the most essential, the typically representative, or as otherwise responsive to perceived needs of the particular type of library" (Introduction). Therefore the lists are not comprehensive; they include 1,547 books, 26 periodicals, 134 films, 38 filmstrips, slides, and transparencies, 47 records, and 4 tapes in the following categories: bibliography and reference, general, fine arts, economics, education, history, literature, philosophy and religion, politics and government, science and technology, social science, folklore, and picture books. The entries are not annotated.

*Arrangement:* Geographical with topical subdivisions, then alphabetical by author or title.

*Entries:* Type of library or collection in code, entry number, author, title, series title, type of medium if nonprint, length, sound or silent, color or b/w, publisher/producer, date, Library of Congress catalog card number if any, price, ISBN number, source in the northwest (for nonprint).

*Special Features:* Index by author, title, series, translator, illustrator, performer, editor, type of medium.

**196. Recommended Non-Stereotyped Software and Educational Materials,** prepared by the Software Committee for the Conference, Sexism in Education, held at Arizona State University, October 1975. Kate MacMullin, Chairperson. College of Education, Arizona State University, Tempe, AZ 85281. Available in microfiche and hard copy from ERIC Document Reproduction Service, P.O. Box 190, Arlington, VA 22210. 1975. Apply for current prices. 10p. ED 121 304.

*Scope:* Approximately 60 titles of filmstrips, cassettes, multimedia kits, packets, photo sets, and records evaluated by the committee and recommended for primary, intermediate, junior high school, high school and adult groups.

*Arrangement:* Alphabetical by title.

*Entries:* Title, type of medium, sound or captioned, publisher/producer/distributor with address, accompanying materials if any, description of content, evaluation, audience or grade level.

*Special Features:* Other resources (not previewed); guides for the improvement of images in resources.

197. **Record and Tape Reviews Index,** by Antoinette O. Maleady. Scarecrow Press, Inc., Box 656, Metuchen, NJ 08840. Volume 1971, published in 1972. $8.50. 234p.; Volume 1972, published in 1973. $13.50. 519p.; Volume 1973, published in 1974, $20. 692p.; Volume 1974, published in 1975. $18.50. 580p.

*Scope:* An index to reviews of classical music and spoken works recorded on discs, tapes, and cassettes, and which appeared in the major reviewing media. Each volume covers releases for the preceding year and is a continuation rather than a cumulation of previous volumes. However, if a title was reviewed in 1974 and was also reviewed in 1973, 1972, and 1971, all of the reviews have been brought together in Volume 1974.

*Arrangement:* In four sections—latest volume: (1) alphabetical by composer; (2) alphabetical by name of manufacturer, for collections of several composers on one tape or disc; (3) alphabetical by title, for anonymous works; (4) alphabetical by performer.

*Entries:* Main entry appears in Section 1. Composer, entry number, title, performer(s), conductor, labels and numbers, number of discs in album or set, variant label number, evaluation rating (by code), source of review.

*Special Features:* Abbreviations for periodicals indexed; abbreviations used for performers; explanation of qualitative evaluation of recordings code.

*Author's Note:* An announcement received in September 1976 reports the following changes in title, scope, publisher, and price beginning with the 1976 issue: *Index to Record and Tape Reviews: A Classical Music Buying Guide,* by A. Maleady. Chulainn Press, P.O. Box 770, San Anselmo, CA 94960. Volume 1975, published in 1976. $35. 635p.

198. **Recordings for Children: A Selected List of Records and Cassettes,** prepared by the Children's and Young Adult Services Section, New York Library Association. 3d ed. Available from the New York Library Association, 60 E. Forty-second St., Suite 1242, New York, NY 10017. 1972. $3 prepaid. 40p.

*Scope:* Approximately 450 highly selected discs and cassettes, both musical and nonmusical, for children ranging in age from preschool to 13 years. "In this list the committee has included recordings which will satisfy a wide range of informational and recreational needs of children, recordings which are appealing as well as high quality" (Foreword). Included are folk and fairy tales, documentaries about people and places and about science and technology, songs, folk music, dance music, operas and operettas, ballet, musical shows and soundtracks, holidays.

*Arrangement:* By category and then alphabetical by album title.

*Entries:* Title, composer/author, performing group, narrator, record label and number, and/or cassette number, brief description, asterisk preceding titles suitable for very young children.

*Special Features:* Index which includes additional subject headings; directory of distributors not listed in *Schwann Record and Tape Guide.*

199. **Records and Cassettes for Young Adults: A Selected List,** prepared by the Children's and Young Adult Services Section, New York Library Association. Available from the New York Library Association, 60 E. Forty-second St., Suite 1242, New York, NY 10017. 1972. $3 prepaid. 52p.

*Scope:* Purposes of this list are "to serve as a buying guide for librarians who wish to start a young adult record or cassette collection or to add to an already established collection, and to serve as an information guide for those librarians who would like to be familiar with all kinds of musical and nonmusical works, their composers, performers, etc., in order to better serve their young adult public" (Introduction). Musical categories include: popular (rock, soul, country, western); folk; jazz, with blues and gospel; musical and movie soundtracks; and classical, including electronic. Nonmusical categories are: comedy; documentary and speeches; instruction—"how-to" records; movie, radio, and stage plays; poetry; short stories and other prose; sound effects.

*Arrangement:* In two broad sections—musical and nonmusical, and then by categories (popular, folk, classical, etc.). Main entries are arranged alphabetically with the record album performer, composer, or writer listed first depending on which seems most useful.

*Entries:* Title, performer, composer, writer (order varies), record label and number, cassette number, annotation.

*Special Features:* How to Use this List; Bibliography.

200. **Reintegrating Mentally Retarded People into the Community: An Annotated Bibliography of Print and Audiovisual Information and Training Materials,** sponsored by the Research and Training Center in Mental Retardation, University of Oregon, Eugene, OR 97403. Available from the Program for the Analysis of Deinstitutionalization Resources, Council for Exceptional Children, 1920 Association Drive, Reston, VA 22091. 1975. Free while supply lasts. 31p. Available also in microfiche and hard copy from ERIC Document Reproduction

Service, P.O. Box 190, Arlington, VA 22210. Apply for current prices. ED 112 534.

*Scope:* An annotated list of 123 print and nonprint references which "document innovating efforts" for reintegrating the mentally retarded into the community (Introduction). The list was compiled from mail surveys, computer searches of national information systems, library handsearches, and a telephone survey of developmental disabilities consultants. Included are books, journal articles, reports, monographs, films, and slide sets. More than half of the entries were published during the period January 1973 to May 1975.

*Arrangement:* In two sections—print and audiovisual inclusions—then alphabetical by title.

*Entries:* Title, author (print), type of medium, date, length in pages/minutes/slides, descriptive annotation, name and address of source.

201. **A Resource Guide on Indian Arts and Crafts for Elementary and Secondary Teachers,** prepared by Madeleine Fagot. Center for Indian Education, College of Education Building, Room 417, Arizona State University, Tempe, AZ 85281. 1974. $1.50. 56p. Available also in microfiche and hard copy from ERIC Document Reproduction Service, P.O. Box 190, Arlington, VA 22210. Apply for current prices. ED 097 154.

*Scope:* This list includes approximately 260 arts and crafts reference materials published or produced during the period 1923–73. In addition to the 129 books are films and filmstrips, maps and charts, picture sets, magazines, bibliographies, indexes, slide kits and transparencies. Among the subject areas covered are sandpainting, weaving, silversmithing, music, pottery, and many other art and craft forms unique to specific tribes or to the American Indian in general.

*Arrangement:* By type of medium. Book section is alphabetical by author; nonprint sections are alphabetical by title, except in a few cases where the section is divided by subject, then alphabetical by title.

*Entries:* Books—author, title, publisher, place, date, number of pages. Other entries—title, series title, type of medium, distributor code number, descriptive annotation, length in minutes/frames, sound or silent, color or b/w, date, price (for some items).

*Special Features:* Distributors' addresses; addresses for supplies; places to write for more information; subject index to the book section.

202. **Resource Materials for Consumer Education: A Revision of a 1972 Edition,** by V. Susan Foxwell. Consumer Protection Section, Alaska Department of Law, in conjunction with the Alaska State Department of Education, Juneau, AK 99801. Available in microfiche and hard copy from ERIC Document Reproduction Service, P.O. Box 190, Arlington, VA 22210. 1974. Apply for current prices. 62p. ED 099 299.

> *Scope:* The resources in this list are designed for students in grades K-12 and include the following categories of media: multimedia, films, filmstrips, slides, pictures, transparencies, booklets, study materials, books, records and tapes, teaching units, guidelines, bibliographies, games and other teaching aids. A majority of the titles are filmstrips and booklets; the entries are not annotated.
> *Arrangement:* By type of medium in the order listed above.
> *Entries:* Title or series title, distributor, grade level, cost, length, color or b/w, developer's purpose when available, accompanying materials if any, individual titles if a series.

203. **Resources for Consumer Education: 16mm Films,** by Nancy B. Greenspan. Center for Consumer Education Services, New Jersey State Department of Education, NJJCC-Building 871, Plainfield Ave., Edison, NJ 08817. 1976. $1. 24p. (The first publication of a *Resources* series replacing *Selected Audio-Visual Materials for Consumer Education,* CCES, 1974. Two additional bibliographies in the series—one on 35mm filmstrips and slides, and one on audio kits, teaching kits and transparencies—are planned for publication in 1977.)

> *Scope:* A comprehensive list of available, nonsponsored 16mm films for consumer education suitable for audiences ranging from pre-kindergarten to adult levels. Subjects included are: consumer behavior, advertising, food/shopping, automobiles, financial management, credit, economic understanding, economic influences (government), social philosophy, shoplifting, protection.
> *Arrangement:* Alphabetical by title.
> *Entries:* Title, date, color or b/w, length, description of content, purchase/rental source with address, purchase and rental prices.
> *Special Features:* A chart which indexes the film titles by audience levels and subjects.

204. **Resources for Teaching Word Identification,** edited by Leo M. Schell, Constance Winters, and Gail Pettit. Published jointly by the College of Education, Kansas State University, Manhattan, KS, and the Kansas Council of the International Reading Association. Available from Professor Leo M. Schell, College of Education, Kansas

State University, Manhattan, KS 66506. 1973. $1. 56p. Available also in microfiche and hard copy from ERIC Document Reproduction Service, P.O. Box 190, Arlington, VA 22210. Apply for current prices. ED 078 377.

*Scope:* A bibliography of audiovisual materials, nonbook practice materials, phonic readers, programmed materials, word analysis programs, workbooks, sources of reading games, activities, and ideas which may contribute to the improvement of reading instruction—developmental, corrective, and remedial—at all levels. Materials for grades 1 through 6 are stressed; there are a few materials suitable for secondary school students and none which are designed specifically for college students. The materials are not evaluated and inclusion in the list does not mean endorsement by the authors.

*Arrangement:* By type of material, then alphabetical by title.

*Entries:* Title, grade level, author (books), description of items in kits/sets/series, teacher's manual if available, producer/publisher.

*Special Features:* Names and addresses of publishers and producers.

205. **Schwann-1 Record and Tape Guide.** Monthly. **Schwann-2 Record and Tape Guide.** Semiannual. W. Schwann, Inc., 137 Newbury St., Boston, MA 02116. Available at most record shops. $1 per monthly issue; 95¢ per semiannual issue. (If unavailable locally, apply to publisher for list of dealers who solicit subscriptions; if not available elsewhere, library, educational, and radio subscriptions are available directly from Schwann)

*Scope: Schwann-1* is a selective reference guide, revised monthly, and currently listing about 45,000 stereo long-playing records, 8-track cartridge tapes, and cassettes on approximately 682 record labels, 237 tape labels, and 85 quadrophonic labels. Categories include: new listings for the month, mono and electronically processed stereo records, classical works, electronic music, collections, musicals and TV shows, pop records, jazz and jazz anthologies. Christmas records appear in the November and December issues. Recordings sold only by direct mail are excluded. *Schwann-2* lists many records and tapes not in *Schwann-1.* Categories include: classical and jazz monos, electronically processed stereos, spoken and miscellaneous (including bird songs, documentary, humor, instruction, language, plays, poetry, prose, railroad sounds, sound effects, test records), international pop and folk records on United States labels, noncurrent popular (including band, Hawaiian, organ, religious).

*Arrangement:* Classical section is alphabetical by composer, then alphabetical by title. Other sections vary—alphabetical by performer(s), by title, by type of music, by country, by label, etc.—featuring main characteristic of the category.

*Entries:* Composer with birth and death dates (for classical entries), title, opus or thematic index number, language, artist(s)/performing group, conductor, record/tape format in code, label and number.

*Special Features:* Recent books on music; record price list; tape price list; alphabetical title/composer list; ballet title list; opera title list.

*Author's Note:* The following separate lists, published at varying intervals, are based on information in *Schwann-1* and *Schwann-2* and are available at record stores or postpaid from the publisher at indicated prices: *Basic Record Library*, a 16-page booklet listing 150 classical selections, 50¢; *Basic Record Library of Jazz*, containing 250 recordings from the 1920s to the mid-1970s, 75¢; *Children's Record and Tape Guide*, published annually in December, 75¢; *Schwann 1976 Artist Issue*, containing classical records and tapes from *Schwann-1* and *Schwann-2* through January 1976, arranged by performing artists in six sections: Orchestras, Quartets, etc.; Conductors; Instrumental Soloists; Choral Groups; Operatic Groups; Vocalists; $3.95 through dealers; $4.50 by mail.

**206. The Seed Catalog: A Guide to Teaching/Learning Materials,** by Jeffrey Schrank. Beacon Press, 25 Beacon St., Boston, MA 02108. 1974. $6.95 paper; $12.95 cloth. 374p.

*Scope:* Thousands of "learning seeds"—people, ideas, free and inexpensive publications, associations, books, films, tapes and records, filmstrips and slides, periodicals, games, videotapes, and devices to provoke and educate are listed in this illustrated catalog designed for educators, community workers, and discussion groups. Some of the topics are: violence, soft architecture, science, home economics, abortion, student rights, supernatural events, how to start your own radio station, death and aging, underground video movement, sexism in children's books, and how to use photography in the classroom. The author states that the catalog is biased in favor of provocative, creative, and controversial material, toward the humanities and communication arts, toward inexpensive learning materials, and toward high school and adult learners, since he feels they have been more neglected in educational reform than children. Items included in the catalog are fully described and critically evaluated; many of them have appeared in past issues of *Media Mix*.

*Arrangement:* By type of medium, then alphabetical by title or pro-
ducing agency.

*Entries:* Title, author/editor, publisher/producer/distributor, catalog number, length in minutes/pages/items, color or b/w, date
(some items), rental/purchase price, descriptive/critical review
ranging from one paragraph to a full page or more.

*Special Features:* Illustrations and catalog-type format.

207. **A Selected Annotated Bibliography of Material Relating to Racism,
Blacks, Chicanos, Native Americans and Multi-Ethnicity.** Division
of Minority Affairs, Michigan Education Association, East Lansing,
MI 48823. Available in microfiche and hard copy from ERIC Document Reproduction Service, P.O. Box 190, Arlington, VA 22210.
1971–75. Apply for current prices. Volume 1, 1971. ED 069 445; Volume 2, 1973. ED 117 230; Volume 3, 1974. ED 117 231; Volume 4,
1975. ED 117 290.

*Scope:* The purpose of this four-part bibliography is to provide classroom teachers and other educators with information about resources that will help foster an appreciation for the plural ethnic-
ity of our society; in addition, the work is intended to serve as a
factor in motivating school districts to modify their curricula to
include ethnic and cultured diversity in each curriculum component. The lists are not intended to be all-inclusive, but to present
that material which is most representative of the realities concerning the involvement and contributions of these minorities to the
development of the United States. In each of the volumes the
entries are listed under five topics: racism, black, Chicano, Native
American, and multiethnic materials. Each part is subdivided by
types of media including films, filmstrips, records, tapes, and
printed materials. Audience levels range from elementary and
high school to professional teacher groups.

*Arrangement:* By the five topics mentioned above, then by type of
medium. Books are arranged alphabetically by author; nonprint
materials, alphabetically by title.

*Entries:* Title or series title, author, publisher/producer/distributor,
date, length, color or b/w, rental/purchase price, individual titles
if a series, evaluative annotation, suggested use, audience level,
subject headings (volume 1).

*Special Features:* A list, "Third World Publishers," appears at the
end of the second volume.

208. **A Selected Annotated Bibliography of Resource Materials for the
Implementation of Career Education, Grades K through 3,** by Kath-

ryn A. Heyel. Vocational-Technical Curriculum Laboratory, Rutgers, The State University, Building 4103, Kilmer Campus, New Brunswick, NJ 08903. 1975. $1.50 plus postage. 112p. (Publication no.0003) Available also in microfiche and hard copy from ERIC Document Reproduction Service, P.O. Box 190, Arlington, VA 22210. Apply for current prices. ED 110 747.

*Scope:* This bibliography for teachers and those preparing for teaching was compiled by searching standard selection tools, publishers catalogs, and educational publications. Resources identified were then listed according to grade levels and the following curriculum units: family jobs, community helpers, school workers, foods, clothing, shelter, schools/maps, recreation, communities, colonial times, community needs, citizenship. Among the 578 entries, 332 are for printed materials and 246 for nonprint—films, motion pictures, filmloops, cassette tapes, study prints and transparencies. Each entry includes the selection tool or catalog in which it was listed and a brief description of content.

*Arrangement:* By grade level, then by curriculum category, then by type of medium (print or nonprint). Print materials are listed alphabetically by author; nonprint items are alphabetical by title.

*Entries:* Author, title, publisher/producer, date, series title, type of medium, length in pages/frames/minutes, color or b/w, sound or silent, price, annotation, selection source in code.

*Special Features:* Key to symbols for media selection aids; summary, findings, conclusions, and recommendations; tables of statistical summaries of materials identified; bibliography.

**209. Selected Audiovisuals on Mental Health.** National Institute of Mental Health, 5600 Fishers Lane, Rockville, MD 20852. Available from the Superintendent of Documents, U.S. Government Printing Office, Washington, DC 20402. 1975. $2.95. 223p. (DHEW Publication no. ADM 76–259) Cover title: *Selected Mental Health Audiovisuals.*

*Scope:* A compilation of abstracts of 2,300 currently available films, filmstrips, audiotapes, and videotapes contained in the computer information system of the National Clearinghouse for Mental Health Information of the National Institute of Mental Health. Subjects include: aging, animal studies, biochemistry and metabolism, child mental health, cognition and perception, community mental health, crime and delinquency, death and suicide, depression, family mental retardation, minority groups, motivation, neurosciences, personality, psychology, religion, schizophrenia, sexology, sleep and dreams, social issues, treatment.

*Arrangement:* Alphabetical by subject, then numerical by abstract accession number assigned to each title.

*Entries:* Abstract accession number, distributor's name and address, rental and/or sales price, title, type of medium, color or b/w, length, date of release, brief descriptive annotation.

*Special Features:* Information concerning the format and use of the catalog; sources for free social welfare films; sources for low-cost film rental; addresses of commercial rental libraries.

210. **A Selected Bibliography for Public Administrators in Minority Settings,** compiled by Bonnie J. Gillespie. Council of Planning Librarians, P.O. Box 229, Monticello, IL 61856. 1974. $1.50. 18p. (Exchange Bibliography no.698) Available also in microfiche and hard copy from ERIC Document Reproduction Service, P.O. Box 190, Arlington, VA 22210. ED 103 566.

*Scope:* "Black, native, and Spanish-speaking Americans are the three main minorities mostly considered in this selected bibliography. ... The fourth minority included herein is women" (Introduction). The types of materials listed are books, periodical articles, films, filmstrips, records, tapes, games, and other media. The entries are not annotated, but the subject arrangement indicates the topics treated in the materials: ethnic and minority groups, urban crisis and development, equity and citizen participation, prison literature and criminal justice, epistemics, values, change and systematic models.

*Arrangement:* By subjects, then by media categories, then alphabetical by author or title.

*Entries:* Author (print), title or series title, type of medium (nonprint), length, color or b/w, publisher/producer/distributor, date (print).

211. **A Selected Bibliography of Films and Videotapes on Foreign Language Teacher Training,** compiled by Peter A. Eddy. Center for Applied Linguistics, ERIC Clearinghouse on Languages and Linguistics, 1611 N. Kent St., Arlington, VA 22209. Available in microfiche and hard copy from ERIC Document Reproduction Service, P.O. Box 190, Arlington, VA 22210. 1975. Apply for current prices. 34p. ED 102 875. (CAL-ERIC/CLL Series on Languages and Linguistics no.8)

*Scope:* The author's purpose in compiling this bibliography for foreign language teacher trainers and curriculum specialists was to present as comprehensive a listing as possible—not an evaluated list. The titles were culled from audiovisual center catalogs and from periodicals in which such materials are advertised, and are grouped into four major categories: foreign language teaching methodology, documentary, promotional materials produced by professional organizations to stimulate foreign language study, and social interaction in the classroom. The first section on methodology is subdivided as follows: English as a second language, French, German, Latin, Russian, and Spanish. The majority of items first appeared in the 1960s and range in level from elementary school through college.

*Arrangement:* By subject categories and subheadings mentioned above, then alphabetical by title.

*Entries:* Title or series title, date when available, color or b/w, type of medium, length, description of content, distributor, rental and purchase prices.

*Special Features:* Addresses of sources.

212. **A Selected Discography of Solo Song: Supplement 1971–1974,** by Dorothy Stahl. Information Coordinators, Inc., 1435–37 Randolph St., Detroit, MI 48226. 1976. $9.50. 99p. (Detroit Studies in Music Bibliography) (Continues the author's *A Selected Discography of Solo Song: A Cumulation through 1971*)

*Scope:* A comprehensive list of solo song recordings released from 1971 through 1974—intended to make accessible to teachers and students vocal works on recordings that can be easily procured.

*Arrangement:* Main body (discography) is alphabetical by composer and under composer, alphabetical by title.

*Entries:* Composer with dates of birth and death, song title, name of artist, recording title and number, item number in this publication.

*Special Features:* Index of song titles and first lines in one alphabetical listing; index to abbreviations used on record labels; record albums indexed by manufacturer.

213. **Selected Films and Filmstrips on Four Ethnic American Minorities; (Afro, Indian, Oriental, and Spanish-Speaking),** by Harry A. Johnson. ERIC Clearinghouse on Information Resources, Stanford Center for Research and Development in Teaching, School of Education, Stanford University, Stanford, CA 94305. 1976. $2; check made payable to Box E must accompany order. 55p. Available also in microfiche and hard copy from ERIC Document Reproduction Service, P.O. Box 190, Arlington, VA 22210. Apply for current prices. ED 116 702.

*Scope:* In this list the focus is on multicultural materials which assist in teaching an appreciation and understanding of differences in others. The films and filmstrips included range in grade level from primary through college and were collected in 1973 and 1974 with final choices made in 1975. Selections were made on the basis of authenticity, suitability for children and youth, and relevance in today's world. Materials considered to be condescending to any ethnic group are not included. "Most of this paper was assembled from a more extensive amount of information which will be published in book form by R.R. Bowker late in 1976" (Introduction). In addition to films and filmstrips, other types of nonprint media, position papers, and additional minorities will be included in the Bowker publication to be entitled *Ethnic American Minorities.*

*Arrangement:* Alphabetical by title within each of the four ethnic headings; films are listed first, followed by filmstrips.

*Entries:* Title or series title, producer/distributor code, date, grade level, length in minutes/frames, color or b/w, individual titles if a series, description of content.

*Special Features:* Producers and distributors with addresses; a list of 16 ERIC documents dealing with ethnic minorities and the media, prepared by the ERIC Clearinghouse on Information Resources.

*Author's Note:* The ERIC Clearinghouse on Information Resources is now located at the School of Education, Syracuse University, Syracuse, NY 13210.

214. **Selected Films for Young Adults 1976,** compiled by the Media Selection and Usage Committee of the Young Adult Services Division, American Library Association, 50 E. Huron St., Chicago, IL 60611. 1976. 10¢ single copies; discounts on quantity orders. 5p.

*Scope:* Thirteen 16mm films released in the United States during 1974 and 1975, selected from titles suggested by school and public librarians and audiovisual specialists across the country. The titles "were chosen, after viewing, on the basis of young adult appeal, but each reviewer and juror also took into consideration the technical quality, subject content, and utilization with different kinds of audiences" (p.1).

*Arrangement:* Alphabetical by title.

*Entries:* Title, producer, running time, purchase price, evaluative annotation.

*Special Features:* YASD Media Selection and Usage Committee members.

215. **Selected Free Materials for Classroom Teachers,** by Ruth H. Aubrey. 5th ed. Fearon Publishers, Inc., 6 Davis Dr., Belmont, CA 94002. 1975. $2.50. 130p. (6th ed. scheduled for fall of 1977)

*Scope:* More than 2,000 units of free instructional materials from 562 sources including print and nonprint media. With the exception of films, each of the free materials has been examined by one or more of the panel of evaluators on the basis of importance, presentation, usefulness, and freedom from undesirable advertising and bias. Subjects include: agriculture, art, business, career education, conservation, language arts, health, home economics, industrial education, mathematics, music, physical education, recreation, safety, science, social science, teacher aids.

*Arrangement:* Alphabetical by subject and under each subject, alphabetical by source.

*Entries:* Source, address, title of unit of instructional material, medium format, availability note (quantity, etc.), grade level.

*Special Features:* Suggestions for ordering free materials: names and addresses of distributors; subject and producer index.

216. **Selected Instructional Materials Judged Relevant to Educational Administration,** edited by James R. Yates. University Council for Educational Administration, 29 W. Woodruff Ave., Columbus, OH 43210. 1972. $3.80. 108p. (Must be ordered by the Code W–24) Available also in microfiche and hard copy from ERIC Document Reproduction Service, P.O. Box 190, Arlington, VA 22210. Apply for current prices. ED 077 076.

*Scope:* A highly selected list of over 100 audiovisual media, predominantly 16mm films, judged to be relevant and of high quality from among more than 1,000 titles evaluated by teams of professors and students of general and special educational administration at seven American universities. Content areas are: communication, education and race, group processes, organizational leadership, administrative techniques, and negotiations.

*Arrangement:* Randomly by title—one entry to a page.

*Entries:* Title, producer and distributor (with addresses), type of medium, time in minutes, color or b/w, purchase/rental prices, approximate time required to obtain, description of purpose and content, supportive supplemental materials if any, statement of relevance/quality/applicability.

*Special Features:* Index by media and content; instructional materials evaluation form used by teams; loose-leaf 8½″ x 11″ format.

217. **Selected Media Reviews: Exceptional Children 1970–1973,** Burton Blatt, Editor; Margery A. MacDonald, Assistant Editor. The Council for Exceptional Children, 1920 Association Dr., Reston, VA 22091. 1973. $4.55. 180p.

*Scope:* A compilation of signed, critical reviews of books, films, tapes, and records concerned with the philosophy and goals, instruction and curriculum, evaluation, psychological and social foundations and administration, and standards for programs dealing with exceptional children. "A number of these reviews first appeared in *Exceptional Children.* Many others have not appeared not because of considerations involving quality of review or importance . . . but merely because of space limitations" (Foreword).

*Arrangement:* By type of medium; book review section is subdivided by subjects mentioned above.

*Entries:* Title, author (books), publisher/producer/distributor, place, date, type of medium (nonprint), length in minutes/number of pages, color or b/w (films), price (for some entries), review, name, and position of reviewer.

*Special Features:* Foreword, "On Reviewing Book Reviews," by Burton Blatt; Introduction, "A View from a Small Boat" (a bibliographic essay on some books outside the field of special education), by Maynard C. Reynolds; indexes to books, films, tapes-records; list of reviewers.

218. **Selected References and Aids for Teaching Animal Science to Students of Agricultural Education,** by Larry E. Miller. Agricultural Education, College of Education, Virginia Polytechnic Institute and State University, Blacksburg, VA 24061, and the Agricultural Education Service, Division of Vocational Education, State Department of Education, Richmond, VA 23216. Available in microfiche and hard copy from ERIC Document Reproduction Service, P.O. Box 190, Arlington, VA 22210. 1973. Apply for current prices. 51p. ED 112 097.

*Scope:* A series of tables listing bulletins and circulars, textbooks, films, filmstrips, slides, and commercial materials (literature, charts, aids) in the following six subject areas: general animal science, beef, dairy, poultry, sheep, and swine. For each entry other than textbooks there is a brief description of content. The materials marked with one asterisk are primarily for students; two asterisks denote materials for teacher use.

*Arrangement:* In six tables by subject category, then by type of medium, followed by titles or authors.

*Entries:* Title, asterisks denoting teacher or student use, type of medium, author, length, color or b/w, brief description of content (except textbooks), date (printed materials only), cost, source.

*Special Feature:* Addresses of relevant educational institution sources, commercial companies, and textbook publishers.

**219.** A Selected Special Education Bibliography and Resource Guide, compiled by Ingrid Draper. The Detroit Pre-School Technical Assistance Resource and Training Center. Available from Physical Education and Recreation for the Handicapped: Information and Research Utilization Center (IRUC), 1201 Sixteenth St., N.W., Washington, DC 20036. 1975. $7.50 photocopy (no.238), 102p. Available also in microfiche and hard copy from ERIC Document Reproduction Service, P.O. Box 190, Arlington, VA 22210. Apply for current prices. ED 121 038.

*Scope:* This guide was prepared to assist Head Start personnel who are not experienced in special education and to provide a listing of current training materials for special educators. Included are: a list of national, state, and local sources of information and resources in each of the major areas of exceptionality; widely used professional journals in the field; lists of printed and free and inexpensive materials concerning mental retardation, speech and hearing disorders, vision, learning disabilities, emotional disturbance, orthopedic and other health impairments, parent education, supportive services, and curriculum strategies; lists and descriptions of educational films, inservice training materials, filmstrips, cassettes, recordings, and videotapes for parents and educators.

*Arrangement:* By subject categories and types of media in the order listed above.

*Entries:* Author (print), title, publisher/producer/distributor, date, rental fee or price (for low cost and nonprint items), description of content, type of medium (nonprint).

*Special Features:* A list of early childhood programs for young handicapped children.

**220.** A Selective Guide to Materials for Mental Health and Family Life Education. 3d ed. Mental Health Materials Center, 419 Park Ave., New York, NY 10016. 1976. $65 hard cover; $52.50 soft cover. 1,000p. (Includes semiannual list of new recommended items)

*Scope:* Approximately 700 items including more than 275 books and pamphlets and more than 225 films and other audiovisual materials are described and critically reviewed in this selected guide to educational media in the fields of mental health and family living. The subjects included are: infancy, early childhood, preadolescence, school mental health, young adults, marriage and family life including sex education, self-understanding, later maturity and aging, alcohol use and abuse, crime and delinquency, drug abuse, mental illness, developmental disabilities in children, mental retardation, physical handicaps, suicide/crisis intervention, intergroup relations, and education for positive mental health. The audience levels range from teen-agers and college groups to professional educators, parents, and parent groups. A new feature in this edition is the identification of materials which are suitable for use in inservice training programs.

*Arrangement:* By subject categories listed above.

*Entries:* Type of medium, title or series title, author (printed materials), publisher/producer, date, length in minutes/pages, summary, individual titles and summaries if a series, evaluation, primary audience, other persons capable of understanding the material, subject category, audiences and uses, ordering information including source and rental/purchase prices.

*Special Features:* "Guidelines for Ordering Publications and Films," "Some Ways of Using Pamphlets in Mental Health and Family Life Education," "Memo to Discussion Leaders," by Nina Ridenour; and the first four chapters of *Mental Health Education: Principles in the Effective Use of Materials,* by Nina Ridenour; comprehensive index.

221. **The Short Film: An Evaluative Selection of 500 Recommended Films,** by George Rehrauer. Macmillan Information, A Division of Macmillan Publishing Co., Inc., 866 Third Ave., New York, NY 10022. 1975. $12.50. 199p.

*Scope:* A total of 36 books on films and 3 issues of one periodical were used by the author in his attempt to distill from among the thousands of films cited a final group of 500 short films (no longer than 60 minutes) addressed to a rather wide range of audiences and limited to films dealing with broad subject fields rather than one discipline or specialty. Each of the films finally selected was recommended by one or more of the book/periodical sources and each film can be used in a variety of ways. A few pre-1950 titles are included, mostly in the field of early documentaries—now accepted classics. The majority of films cited are from the sixties "because films of the seventies have not had their greatest impact as yet" for reasons which the author explains in the introduction. Some of the subjects are: adolescent, Africa, allegory, animal life, animation, anthropology, art, Asia, astronomy, Australia, automobiles, automation, biography, biology, Black studies, Canada, child study (behavior), children's films, city life, communication, drugs, ecology, education, entertainment, family, film as art, France, future, Germany, the handicapped, history, India, Indians (American), labor/industry/workers, literature (children's), mental health, music, Naziism, parables, physiology, prejudice, psychology, religion, satire, social problems, sociology, sports/physical education, technology, twentieth century, war/peace, water/seas/ lakes.

*Arrangement:* Alphabetical by title.

*Entries:* Title (in English), release date, producer/distributor, length, animation, without dialogue, color or b/w, annotation or description, suggested audience, suggested areas of use, recommendation sources (code).

*Special Features:* List of distributors; subject headings; film titles arranged alphabetically under subjects; illustrations from the films; a bibliography of 36 books about films; other sources of short film information; selected film periodicals which deal with the short film.

222. **Social Factors in Health Care: An Evaluation of Selected Films and Videotapes,** by Gerard J. Hunt and Allen S. Mondell. Department of Psychiatry, School of Medicine, University of Maryland, 645 W. Redwood St., Baltimore, MD 21201. $2 (check payable to Gerard J. Hunt). 63p.

*Scope:* The 40 titles of films and videotapes in this guide were selected and evaluated in an effort "to help medical students learn about the social and cultural factors which bear upon health and the practice of medicine" (Introduction). Divided into two parts, titles in the first part of the list deal with the current crises in health care delivery in the United States and efforts toward solutions; the second part presents materials in areas with significant social implications including such topics as birth, death, alcoholism, drug abuse, suicide, aging, and the prevention of illness.

*Arrangement:* Alphabetical by title under two broad subject categories: delivery of health services, and problem areas in medical care.

*Entries:* Title, date, producer, distributor and address, rental/purchase price, length, color or b/w, sound or silent, synopsis, general evaluation including suggested audiences.

*Special Features:* Sources of films and other audiovisual material; outline for a course in medical sociology offered by Dr. Gerard Hunt in the School of Medicine, University of Maryland, spring of 1972.

223. **Songs of Protest, War, & Peace: A Bibliography & Discography,** by R. Serge Denisoff. American Bibliographical Center-Clio Press, Inc., 2040 Alameda Serra, Santa Barbara, CA 93103. 1973. $3.75. 70p. (War/Peace Bibliography Series developed in cooperation with the Center for the Study of Armament and Disarmament, California State University, Los Angeles)

*Scope:* In this series, each issue is intended to provide a comprehensive "working," rather than definitive, bibliography on a relatively narrow theme within the spectrum of war/peace studies. This issue includes not only protest songs and discs (over 200 titles), but also lists of books and periodicals and literature on the radical right's attack upon protest songs. The introductory comment provides an assessment of the role of music in American antiwar movements from the Revolutionary War to 1973. "The bibliographical and discographical material . . . in part, has been compiled in order to stimulate further research in an area which has generally received very little study" (Introduction).

*Arrangement:* Alphabetical by author or composer under broad subject headings.

*Entries:* Author/composer, title, source/publisher/label and number, date.

*Special Features:* Explanation of abbreviations used; index.

224. **Sound Recordings in the Audiovisual Division of the National Archives,** by Mayfield S. Bray and Leslie C. Waffen. National Archives and Records Service, Washington, DC 20408. Available in microfiche and hard copy from ERIC Document Reproduction Service, P.O. Box 190, Arlington, VA 22210. 1972. Apply for current prices. 30p. ED 081 240.

*Scope:* Approximately 47,000 sound recordings of press conferences, panel discussions, interviews, speeches, court and conference proceedings, entertainment programs, and news broadcasts have been collected in the National Archives and are listed in this paper. Although many items were received from private sources, most are from the records of about 65 federal government agencies. The Audiovisual Archives Division furnishes reproductions of these records, subject in some cases to copyright and/or restrictions imposed by the agency of transfer or the donor.

*Arrangement:* By federal government agency.

*Entries:* Name of agency, record number, date, number of items, description of content.

*Special Features:* Appendix 1, An Index to Persons Whose Voices Are Known to Be Recorded in the Holdings; Appendix 2, An Index to Radio Series on Special Programs.

225. **Spoken Records,** by Helen Roach. 3d ed. Scarecrow Press, Inc., Box 656, Metuchen, NJ 08840. 1970. $8.50. 288p.

*Scope:* More than 500 spoken recordings are critically reviewed in this work, including documentaries, lectures, and interviews; readings by authors (Robert Frost, T. S. Eliot, W. B. Yeats, William Faulkner, and others); readings by other than authors in English, American, Scottish, Irish; children's literature; religious and biblical works; and plays of Shakespeare and others.

*Arrangement:* By subject categories, then alphabetical by title.

*Entries:* Title, producer/distributor, size and number of recordings, label and number. A critical annotation is given in the main text.

*Special Features:* Title index; selected discography of Shakespeare's plays and company addresses of Shakespeare recordings; in addition to the Shakespeare discography there is a basic discography of 40 spoken records selected on the basis of excellence, and described in detail in appropriate chapters; Appendix 1, Data of Historic and Human Interest which Became Available During the Study of *Spoken Records;* Appendix 2, Supplementary List of Spoken Records; addresses of record companies cited.

*Author's Note:* Although not revised since 1970, this work is included because it describes several items of historic and lasting value.

226. **Superfilms: An International Guide to Award-Winning Educational Films,** by Salvatore J. Parlato, Jr. Scarecrow Press, Inc., Box 656, Metuchen, NJ 08840. 1976. $13.50. 365p.

*Scope:* "The purpose of this book is to provide a starting point for the selection of better than average films. As such, this directory is quality-oriented—the only known attempt to identify superior films on a large scale" (Preface). Included are approximately 1,500 award-winning productions; the number of festivals listed totals 255 ranging in locale "all the way from Ann Arbor to Zabreb." Among the 105 subject categories represented are: acupuncture, Africa, agriculture, alcoholism, animals, anthropology, art, Australia, biography, biology, birds, Black studies, Canada, careers, chemistry, consumerism, crime and punishment, dance, drugs, energy, Eskimo life, evaluation, film techniques, the handicapped, holidays, humor, India, Israel, Latin America, life and death, Mexico, Middle East, minorities, nutrition, physics, poetry, pollution, race relations, Russia, sculpture, seasons, sex education, solar system, teaching, transportation, urban living, venereal disease, war and peace, women's studies, The film descriptions are based on producers' notes.

*Arrangement:* Film descriptions—alphabetical by title.

*Entries:* Title, running time, color or b/w, distributor, date, award/ prize/medal, name and location of festival, description, producer, audience level.

*Special Features:* Subject index categories; programming guide (topical index); film festivals and competitions including name or level of awards and the location if known; company-title index; film companies with addresses and abbreviations.

227. **Systems Film Catalog.** Association for Systems Management, 24587 Bagley Road, Cleveland, OH 44138. [1973]. $3. 60p.

*Scope:* An annotated list of approximately 300 16mm films on the following subjects: communications, data processing, human relations, management, office management, systems applications, work simplification and improvement, general.
*Arrangement:* By subject categories listed above, then alphabetical by title.
*Entries:* Title, description of content, producer, color or b/w, running time, source(s), rental price(s).
*Special Features:* Film sources; alphabetical title index.

228. **Teacher's Resource Handbook for Latin American Studies: An Annotated Bibliography of Curriculum Materials, Preschool through Grade Twelve,** by John N. Hawkins. Published with the assistance of the Curriculum Inquiry Center at the University of California, Los Angeles. UCLA Latin American Center Publications, 405 Hilgard Ave., Los Angeles, CA 90024. 1975. $2.50. 220p. (UCLA Latin American Center Reference Series v.6)

*Scope:* This comprehensive bibliography is part of a long-term project to design and implement instructional materials for teaching about Latin America at the precollegiate level. Types of materials included are books, films, filmstrips, records, slides, tapes, transparencies, multimedia kits, posters, and pictures. The materials were produced during the period 1969–75 and most were not seen or evaluated by the staff. Therefore, two model evaluation forms are included which are designed to assist teachers in assessing the quality of the cross-cultural content of the materials.
*Arrangement:* By grade levels, by geographic region, then by type of medium, followed by titles in alphabetical order.
*Entries:* Title or series title, author, date, length, color or b/w, sound or silent, individual titles if a collection or series, publisher/producer/distributor, price, brief description, asterisk denoting title has been seen and annotated by a staff member.
*Special Features:* Materials Assessment Sheet; Cross-Cultural Evaluation Sheet; bibliographies and additional sources; publishers and distributors.

229. **Teaching about the Law,** by Ronald A. Gerlach and Lynne W. Lamprecht. The W. H. Anderson Co., 646 Main St., Cincinnati, OH 45201. 1975. $9.95. 354p.

*Scope:* A resource book for social studies teachers in grades K-12 which discribes objectives, goals, learning activities, teaching techniques, and a variety of instructional materials and other resources for implementing law education programs in the classroom. In addition to the chapter which describes and evaluates currently available printed materials, there is a chapter which identifies, evaluates, and suggests appropriate uses for films, filmstrips, feature films, pictures and photographs, recordings, slide kits, transparencies, and video programs. There are also discursive bibliographies of professional materials for teachers, legal reference materials, case studies, and descriptions of community resources and such techniques as simulation, role playing, gaming, evaluation and clarification strategies.

*Arrangement:* By subject and type of medium.

*Entries:* Title or series title, publisher/producer, annotation, individual titles if a series, length, distributor or source.

*Special Features:* General index.

230. **Teaching Africa Today: A Handbook for Teachers and Curriculum Planners,** by E. Jefferson Murphy and Harry Stein. School Services Division, African-American Institute, 833 United Nations Plaza, New York, NY 10017. Published by Citation Press, Scholastic Magazines, Inc., 50 W. Forty-fourth St., New York, NY 10036. 1973. $3.95. 285p.

*Scope:* This handbook is designed to assist educators in the preparation of curricula on African studies for students in grades K-12 and to contribute to the improvement of classroom teaching in this field. The basic concepts, themes, and issues are discussed throughout the text, followed by selected and annotated lists of films, filmstrips, maps, slides, transparencies, and printed materials recommended for teaching. African subjects included are geography, history, political and economic development of the nations, social and cultural development of the nations, Africa's relations with the United States and with the rest of the world, the dilemma of South Africa. "The staff of the School Services Division of the African-American Institute, educators with extensive experience in African and American schools have spent years collecting and evaluating materials on Africa as well as discussing with teachers their utility in the classroom. The lists in this handbook represent their authoritative judgments on what are the most reliable and useful" (Introduction).

*Arrangement:* By topics in the order listed above, then by type of medium divided into Teacher References and Classroom Use categories.

*Entries:* Title or series title, author, producer/publisher/distributor and address, length in minutes/pages/number of items, color or b/w, date, related materials if any, individual titles if a series, rental/sales price, recommended grade level, descriptive and evaluative annotation.

*Special Features:* Introduction: on teaching about Africa and suggested course outlines; guidelines for selecting curriculum materials; visual/media resources; major commercial sources; film rental libraries; sources of free films; brief list of filmographies.

231. **Teaching Materials Currently Used in Mental Health Worker Training Programs,** sponsored by the Southern Regional Education Board, Atlanta, GA 30301. Available in microfiche and hard copy from ERIC Document Reproduction Service, P.O. Box 190, Arlington, VA 22210. 1974. Apply for current prices. 113p. ED 103 043.

*Scope:* A selective list of teaching resources commonly used and found to be most valuable by faculty of approximately 175 college programs that are preparing mental health or human service technicians at the Associate of Arts level. The information was put together by a task force sponsored by the Southern Regional Education Board. Categories included are: books, journals and journal articles, films and filmstrips, consultants and general resources, and miscellaneous. The annotations include not only descriptions of content but also critical comments indicating special limitations, if any.

*Arrangement:* By categories for resources in the order listed above.

*Entries:* Title, author (print), publisher/producer, date, code indicating uses, number of persons using the item, length, color or b/w, price, annotation and critical comments.

*Special Features:* Categorical index; alphabetical subject index; Appendix A, Task Force Roster; Appendix B, Evaluative Response Sheet.

232. **Themes Two: One Hundred Short Films for Discussion,** by William Kuhns. Cebco Standard Publishing, Cebco Pflaum, 9 Kulick Rd., Fairfield, NJ 07006. 1974. $5.95. 193p. (A sequel to the author's *Themes: Short Films for Discussion,* 1969)

*Scope:* The 100 critically-annotated films were selected from over 200 shorts screened by the author and are on the following themes: absurdist, aggression, allegorical, animation technique, biographical, childhood, the city, companionship, competition,

dance, death, dehumanization, documentary, education, environment, film history, film technique, future, graphics and motion
graphics films, history, humor, illusion, initiative, literary or folk
source, media, music, patriotism, politics, population, power and
authority, repression, romanticism, satirical and spoof, sexual conflict, sport, technology, time, totalitarianism, violence, war. Almost
all of the films are animation, approximately a dozen are totally
abstract graphic films, and with a few exceptions, all films are less
than an hour long—most are fewer than 10 minutes.

*Arrangement:* Alphabetical by title.

*Entries:* Title, country, production date, length, color or b/w, direc-
tor/author/designer, producer, distributor, descriptive/critical annotation a page or more in length.

*Special Features:* Annotated list of distributors; annotated bibliography; thematic index.

233. **Those Oldies but Goodies: A Guide to 50's Record Collecting,** by
S. Propes. The Macmillan Co., 866 Third Ave., New York, NY 10022.
1973. $5.95; $1.95 paper. 192p.

*Scope:* According to the introduction, this work is the first systematic
attempt to describe and define those elements that constitute a
valid collection of 1950s music. The book is directed not only to
the established collector, "but also and especially to the person
with enough interest in early rock and roll and rhythm and blues
originals to assemble a personal collection of this important art
form". (Introduction). In the opening chapters, the author describes the nature of rare records, the record labels, and the pre-
dominant themes of the 50s. The discographies in the succeeding
chapters of the book are preceded by a discussion of the history,
sound, rarity, and value of the records listed.

*Arrangement:* By type of music followed by performing groups and
individuals.

*Entries:* Label and number, title, date.

*Special Features:* Sources; brief list of related publications.

234. **Training Film Profiles.** Olympic Media Information, 71 W. Twenty-
third St., New York, NY 10010. Bimonthly. 1968 to date. Apply for
current prices and subscription rates. 8½" x 11" loose-leaf format
with one entry per page. (Cumulative index and sample pages free
on letterhead request)

*Scope:* A comprehensive service which identifies, describes, and evaluates approximately 300 films, filmstrips, media kits, cartridge
films and sound-slide programs each year, available from commercial and noncommercial sources. Subjects covered are: prevoca-

tional concepts, employee training, finding a job, performance on the job, communication skills, human relations, guidance and counseling, training the disadvantaged, administrative skills, leadership, consumer education, study skills, continuing education, job enrichment, management, instructor training, values, contemporary culture, and similar areas for personal self-development. Each profile gives complete mediagraphic data, a factual description of the item, its primary audience, a detailed synopsis written by a specialist, discussion questions, related materials, and an objective evaluation. At the close of each volume there is a cumulative title and subject index to all volumes.

*Arrangement:* By subject categories.

*Entries:* Title, subject area, length, type of medium, color or b/w, date, primary audience, content and treatment, components (kits), synopsis, discussion questions, related materials, evaluation, name and address of distributor who rents/sells/loans the item.

*Special Feature:* Loose-leaf format with binders; volumes are completely revised three years after initial publication.

235. **Urban Problems: A Bibliography of Non-Print and Audio-Visual Materials for a Secondary School Geography Course, Supplement to Exchange Bibliography Number 196,** by Charles Bryfogle. Council of Planning Librarians, P.O. Box 229, Monticello, IL 61856. 1972. $6.50. 64p. (Exchange Bibliography no.259)

*Scope:* A list of maps, filmstrips, filmloops, slides, multimedia kits, records, tapes, and transparencies produced in the United States and Canada. Categories included are: basic works, historical works, urbanization as planning, cities as architecture, transportation, society/culture and the city, morphology of the city, pollution, population, cybernetics and society. Annotations are descriptive and evaluative with comments ranging from "superb," "a must," "decidedly useful," to "poor," "of limited value."

*Arrangement:* Audiovisual materials are listed under name and address of producer/distributor, then randomly by title or series/set title. There are separate categories for maps, organizations, indexes, and research projects.

*Entries:* Title or series/set title, catalog order number, type of medium, length in frames/slides/records/pages, color or b/w, price in Canadian and U.S. dollars, descriptive-evaluative comments.

236. **USTA Tennis Film List, 1976,** compiled and edited by Julia Rudy. USTA Education and Research Center, United States Tennis Association Publications, 71 University Place, Princeton, NJ 08540. 1976. $1.50 plus 50¢ postage. 43p. Revised annually.

*Scope:* Described in the preface as "a comprehensive index to over 100 tennis films" the list includes predominantly 16mm films as well as 8mm, super-8mm, filmloops, and videotapes available from commercial distributors, film libraries, and other sources. The entries are categorized as instructional, entertaining, or historic.

*Arrangement:* By type of medium, then by category, then alphabetical by title.

*Entries:* Title, date, brief description, length, color or b/w, sound, format if other than 16mm, purchase and rental sources with prices.

*Special Features:* Directory of USTA regional libraries and free loan libraries; distributor address list; brief information about USTA.

237. **The Video Bluebook: 1975–76 Edition,** edited by Patricia Goff. Co-published by Knowledge Industry Publications, Inc., and Esselte, Inc. Available from Unipub, Box 433, Murray Hill Station, New York, NY 10016, or from Knowledge Industry Publications, Inc., 2 Corporate Park Dr., White Plains, NY 10604. 1975. $29.50 if prepaid; postage added if billed. 368p.

*Scope:* Designed to meet the needs of business, industry, and government for information concerning the availability of video software. The directory was compiled with the cooperation of approximately 95 North American video publishers. The programs cover a wide variety of subjects; among the 5,000 titles listed, 3,500 are aimed at business and 1,500 programs are of general interest and should be of interest also to users in business, industry, and government.

*Arrangement:* Alphabetical by subject.

*Entries:* Subject area, title, series title, publisher(s), production date(s), color or b/w, length of tape, type(s) of tape format(s) available, brief description of program content including individual titles in series or sets, order number(s), preview availability, source, rental and/or sale price(s), special conditions if any.

*Special Features:* Listing of program publishers, including their sales offices; alphabetical listing of program titles, series titles, individual titles in series, and titles of sets; listing of companies which provide services for the video industry.

238. **The Videoplay Program Catalog: For ¾-Inch "U" Videocassettes.** 2d ed. C. S. Tepfer Publishing Co., Inc., 607 Main St., Ridgefield, CT 06877. 1973. $3. 127p.

*Scope:* "This program catalog is a complete guide to the more than 4,100 programs currently available for the machines marketed by Sony, Panasonic, JVC, Concord, and Wollensak" (Title page). The programs deal with a wide subject range and are recommended for preschool to postgraduate levels. Descriptive annotations are included in the Program Title Index section, with other sections providing access to the materials by subjects, key words, and sources.

*Arrangement:* Alphabetical by title.

*Entries:* Title, length, recommended level or use, description of content, producer, date, source, order number, sale and rental prices, clearances, restrictions, associated materials, subject headings.

*Special Features:* "For Your Entertainment," a section of selected titles for home use; subject index; source index; colored paper used to differentiate sections of the catalog.

239. **War. Peace. Film Guide,** by Lucy Dougall. Rev. ed. World Without War Publications, 110 S. Dearborn St., Suite 820, Chicago, IL 60603. 1973. $1.50. 123p. Available also in microfiche only from ERIC Document Reproduction Service, P.O. Box 190, Arlington, VA 22210. Apply for current price. ED 075 310.

*Scope:* The 200 films included in this revised and expanded edition were selected from more than 500 titles which were previewed from 1969 to midsummer 1972. "No single film in this guide speaks to all the dimensions of the problem of ending war. The films are divided into the categories, which, taken together, constitute a body of thought which could help end war" (Introduction). These subjects are: armament and disarmament, international law, international organizations, nonviolent social change, world community, and world development. The list includes feature films as well as 16mm films, films for children as well as adults, animated and experimental films, short films and documentaries. In addition to films are model study units, sample film programs, study guides, specialized catalogs of films, film periodicals, books for children, and a selected bibliography of background readings.

*Arrangement:* Alphabetical by title under broad categories.

*Entries:* Title, date, running time, color or b/w, director/producer/distributor(s) code, price, descriptive/critical annotation including effectiveness, weaknesses, uses, appropriate audience(s).

*Special Features:* Subject index; title index, key to film sources; comments about the author.

240. **With Liberty and Justice for All: A Selected Bibliography.** Division of Equal Educational Opportunity, Indiana Department of Public Instruction, Indianapolis, IN 46204. Available in microfiche and hard copy from ERIC Document Reproduction Service, P.O. Box 190, Arlington, VA 22210. 1975. Apply for current prices. 49p. ED 120 751.

*Scope:* A selected list of printed materials, films, filmstrips, games, records, slides, tapes and cassettes for use in promoting multi-ethnic education. Emphasis is placed on the three major minority groups living in Indiana—the African American, the American Indian, and the Spanish-speaking American. Materials are listed under three categories: the historical, educational, legal, sociological and emotional issues surrounding desegregation; background material about ethnic lifestyles to aid teachers in understanding or knowing about cultures different from their own; and multi-ethnic classroom materials for suggested grade levels. "Because so much of the information about ethnic minorities used in classrooms is inaccurate, or presented from a perspective alien (and often hostile) to the minority group being presented, it was deemed necessary to have scholars who were themselves a member of the particular group select the materials about their own group" (Introduction to part 3).

*Arrangement:* By three broad subject categories mentioned above, then by subtopic and by type of material.

*Entries:* Author (print), title, type of medium (nonprint), publisher/producer/distributor, rental fee or price, descriptive and critical comments, lowest suitable grade level.

*Special Features:* Sources and addresses.

241. **Womanhood Media Supplement: Additional Current Resources about Women,** by Helen R. Wheeler. Scarecrow Press, Inc., P.O. Box 656, Metuchen, NJ 08840. 1975. $15 plus shipping charge. 482p. A supplement to the author's *Womanhood Media: Current Resources About Women,* 1972. $8.50.

*Scope:* An addition to the original volume, which included both print and nonprint resources published or produced, for the most part, before 1971. The *Supplement* omits certain sections of the basic volume (A Women's Liberation Awareness Inventory, Documentation for Human Equality, and Relevant Out-of-Print Titles) and consists mainly of three greatly expanded sections: a basic book collection, nonbook resources, and a directory of sources. "Some areas of concern which receive more consideration in the *Supplement* are affirmative action, the arts, Canadiana, Latinas, Lesbiana, and the media. As a resource, the *Womenhood Media Supplement* can nonetheless be used independently of the basic volume" (Introduction).

*Arrangement:* Basic book collection—Dewey Decimal Classification number, then alphabetical by author; audiovisual resources—alphabetical by title.

*Entries:* For books—author, title, publisher, date, pages, Library of Congress catalog card number, price, descriptive/critical annotations; for nonbook media—title, type of medium, producer and/or distributor, date, length (minutes, frames, parts), color or b/w, rental and/or purchase price, descriptive annotation.

*Special Features:* Index to the basic book collection; directory of sources which lists speakers and consultants, government commissions and councils on the status of women, women's liberation groups and centers, rosters for employment and other affirmative action.

242. **Women and Film: A Resource Handbook,** prepared by the Project on the Status and Education of Women, Association of American Colleges, 1818 R St., N.W., Washington, DC 20009. Available in microfiche and hard copy from ERIC Document Reproduction Service, P.O. Box 190, Arlington, VA 22210. 1974. Apply for current prices. 26p. ED 085 034.

*Scope:* This handbook was prepared "in response to the need for a summary of the media resources available concerning women" (p. 1). The opening pages contain suggestions for planning and for reducing the costs of a film festival focusing on women. The lists which follow include: feature length films pertinent to women's roles, films shown at the first international festival of women's films, short films, slide programs, other resources.

*Arrangement:* By categories mentioned above, then by subtopics. Feature films are listed by decade and title.

*Entries:* Title, date, length in minutes, color or b/w, filmmaker/producer/director, source with address, comments.

243. **Women in Focus,** by Jeanne Betancourt. Cebco Standard Publishing, Cebco Pflaum, 9 Kulick Rd., Fairfield, NJ 07006. 1974. $10. 186p.

*Scope:* A highly selected, critically annotated list of 90 films which are considered to be nonsexist; many of the films were produced by women filmmakers. The author, a film teacher in an all-girls high school, screened all of the films one or more times and used many of them with her students. In the introduction she discusses her criteria for selection, the chief characteristics of films about women, and ways in which the films can be used most effectively in teaching. Each film review is followed by a list of related film titles and by suggested femininst readings. Among the themes treated in the films are: abortion, childbirth, friendship, discrimination, growing up, homesexuality, middle age, marriage, old age, women on welfare, parent-child relationships, pregnancy, prostitution, rape, religion, sex education, self-defense, teen years, careers, violence, women in other cultures, black women, Spanish women. The text is illustrated with photographs of some of the filmmakers and scenes from the films.

*Arrangement:* Alphabetical by title.

*Entries:* Title, description of content, evaluation, excerpts from reviews, date, length, color or b/w, rental and purchase prices, filmmaker, distributor, filmography, suggested feminist readings.

*Special Features:* Illustrations; indexes to titles, filmmakers, and themes; annotated bibliography of books; list of distributors.

244. **Women's Films: A Critical Guide.** Audio-Visual Center, Indiana University, Bloomington, IN 47401. 1975. $5.95. 121p.

*Scope:* A catalog of 172 critically evaluated films selected, for the most part, by evaluation teams representing a cross section of the university communities at Bloomington, Indiana, and Berkeley, California. The list is not intended to be comprehensive, but it includes films on a wide range of subjects, e.g., abortion, problem pregnancies, rape, welfare, jobs, job discrimination, child care, working mothers, self-defense, socialization, and third world women. Also, there are film portraits, documentaries, personal statements, and historical studies.

*Arrangements:* Alphabetical by title in four main sections—film notes (the titles evaluated at Bloomington); film notes from EMC One-73 (Berkeley); films from the Indiana University Audio-Visual Center; recent film releases.

*Entries:* Title, length, color or b/w, purchase price (also rental if from Indiana University), long descriptive/critical annotation, date, distributor, producers.

*Special Features:* Sample film evaluation form; film ordering information; bibliography of books and articles about women; introductory statement "defining women's films"; a title index, and a distributor index.

245. **Women's Films in Print: An Annotated Guide to 800 16mm Films by Women,** compiled by Bonnie Dawson. Booklegger Press, 555 Twenty-ninth St., San Francisco, CA 94131. 1975. $4. 165p.

*Scope:* A list of 800 films by 370 women filmmakers; the productions range chronologically from "Salome" made in 1922 to films released in mid-1975. Only 16mm films available for rent or sale are included. The term made "by women" refers to films produced or directed by women, including some films on which men have collaborated. Canadian women filmmakers are omitted because their work is documented elsewhere. The films cover a wide variety of subjects, not necessarily about women, and represent many types and styles—documentaries, full length features, cartoons, animation using mosaic cutouts, live action pixillation, hand-painted films, etc. The annotations, which summarize or characterize the films rather than evaluate them, were gathered in part from the author's viewings, from the filmmakers, and from distributors' catalogs and film festival programs.

*Arrangement:* Alphabetical by filmmaker's last name, then alphabetical by title.

*Entries:* Filmmaker, title, date made, collaborator, length in minutes, color or b/w, silent or sound, rental/purchase price, distributor(s), annotation and its source.

*Special Features:* Distributors' addresses; bibliography; title index; subject index.

*Author's Note:* A Booklegger Press publication received after the cut-off date for inclusion, *Positive Images, A Guide to Non-Sexist Films for Young People* ($5. 120p.), critically evaluates 400 films, videotapes, slide shows, and filmstrips.

# Index

This index includes references to authors, publishers, organizations, institutions, subjects, types of media, and those titles which are mentioned in the annotations but which are not main entry titles; the latter are omitted because they are alphabetically arranged in the text. Comprehensive indexes and reviewing services which include almost all subjects are given only general subject headings. The term *Multimedia* is used for guides which include two or more types of media. Reference is made to entry numbers, not to page numbers.